You Can't TEACH a Class You Can't MANAGE

by Donna Whyte

D1303871

Crystal Springs BOOKS

A division of
SDE Staff Development for Educators
Peterborough, New Hampshire

Published by Crystal Springs Books
A division of Staff Development for Educators (SDE)
10 Sharon Road, PO Box 500
Peterborough, NH 03458
1-800-321-0401
www.crystalsprings.com
www.sde.com

Published 2008
Printed in the United States of America
12 11 10 09 08   1 2 3 4 5

ISBN: 978-1-934026-10-6

Library of Congress Cataloging-in-Publication Data

Whyte, Donna, 1962-
    You can't teach a class you can't manage / by Donna Whyte.
        p.   cm.
    ISBN 978-1-934026-10-6
    1. Classroom management. I. Title.

    LB3013.W494 2008
    371.102'4--dc22

                                                    2007039004

Editor: Sharon Smith
Art Director and Designer: Soosen Dunholter
Production Coordinator: Jill Shaffer
Illustrator: Mary Ruzicka

This book is dedicated to my daughter, Taylor, and son, Carter, who are challenged to make large and small choices each day of their lives. May they choose to follow their hearts and strive to make the best choices they can.

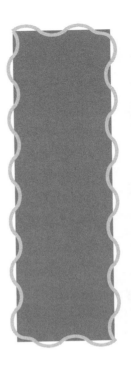

CONTENTS

ACKNOWLEDGMENTS

Several years ago, Lorraine Walker asked me to write this book. She saw the value of sharing the information before I saw it myself, and it was her wish to see me put my thoughts on paper to share with teachers. With heartfelt thanks I say, "I am glad you gave me the nudge to finally communicate the ideas that I believe can change children's lives."

Is This Education or Crowd Control?

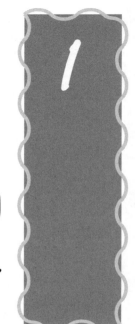

My career in education began in a second-grade classroom. I remember vividly my excitement that summer as I began to plan for and organize what would become my first classroom. Now that I was finally out of college, I was ready to help my new class learn all they needed to know. My classroom was going to be a place of great joy, much fun, and so many opportunities that all the children would succeed. I would impart my vast knowledge; they would attend and learn. It was going to be wonderful.

Reality hit quickly. As I finished my first week, I realized that all my plans and hopes for the learning environment were being overshadowed by the constant demands of managing the class and the children. By the end of the first month, I was questioning my decision to become a teacher. The situation was overwhelming and disheartening. I wondered if I really belonged in a classroom where nothing ever seemed to

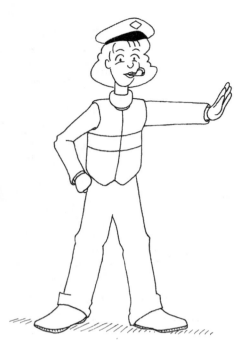

go as planned and everything seemed out of control. In those days, I often described my role as "crowd-control officer." It was not a happy time!

Sadly, this dilemma is shared by many, many teachers. We become educators because we want to "make a difference," but we're not able to make our wonderful visions a reality because we don't have some important behavior management skills. The inability to "control" the class overshadows the dream of being a great teacher. Management issues become a cloud that rains on our parade.

In addition, we worry that these issues will affect how the administration, our colleagues, parents, and even the children view us. And we have cause to worry. Discipline problems are cited as a top reason why administrators decide against rehiring teachers or granting tenure. Teachers who are still on the job cite discipline issues as a big source of stress. Those who have left the field often list discipline problems among the reasons they decided to give up teaching.

What causes this? I'm convinced that two major problems have got us to this point.

The first is that too few teachers really understand discipline. When we get out of college, we've had a lot of education courses and we're dying to get into the classroom, but we're not ready to deal with the children who seem not to want to be taught. We didn't get a lot of college courses on that!

The second issue is that so many people view discipline as a negative thing. We tend to associate it with punishment and to think of it as a drain on the time and energy that should be spent on learning.

I prefer to blame all our challenges on the full moon, Martians, and lack of chocolate for teachers.

But what if discipline were a *positive* thing, an opportunity to teach important life lessons? What if we stopped making assumptions about what children *should* know and do when they come to us? What if we started focusing on *teaching* appropriate behavior?

It's easy to blame society for what's happening to our schools and to our children. There's just too much of too many things: too much TV, too much violence, too much inappropriate language, too much stress, too many food additives. And there's too little of other things: too little family structure, too little extended family nearby, too little time to spend with our children. We could point out plenty of other problems, too. I prefer to blame all our challenges on the full moon, Martians, and lack of chocolate for teachers. In truth, I'm sure that all our discipline problems come from a combination of factors, but in the end, the situation is what it is. Let's not place blame. Let's find solutions.

Time has taught me that during that early period in my career, I wasn't really questioning my commitment and love of teaching. The real issue was my ability to teach in a classroom that was so hard to manage, so "out of control."

Back then, each day was a struggle, and each night I went to bed wondering what I could do to make it better. I believed that the answer lay within me. It took time for me to admit that I couldn't do it alone, that changing the situation would take a commitment on the part of every person (big and small) in the room. What I finally realized, and what I had to teach my stu-

Every child deserves to be given new opportunities for growth that allow her to continue on her path even when she has detoured from it.

dents, was that every person is responsible for his own behavior. That included me, but I was just one piece of the puzzle. Eventually, I understood that I couldn't teach in a classroom that I didn't know how to manage. Management of a classroom is the essential foundation of teaching and learning.

In the beginning, I believed that I could change the situation, but that's not how it works. Reality dictates that communities of learners work as teams. It takes all the members of the team, working together, to build a foundation and keep the group strong. By the way, did you notice? That's not a negative! I believe that helping children to find their love of learning and take internal control of their lives is one of the most satisfying things a teacher can do.

As I write this book, my deepest hope is that I will be able to convey what I have learned about managing and disciplining children—concepts I'm truly passionate about—to other teachers who may struggle with those issues. Every child has the right to learn, the right to be understood, the right to a caring environment, and the right to guidance that will enable that child to become all that he can be. More important, every child deserves to be given new opportunities for growth that allow her to continue on her path even when she has detoured from it.

The Trouble with Understanding "Troublemakers"

I have presented teacher seminars on "positive discipline" for the past five years. This experience has given me insight into a phenomenon that I never knew existed: school "troublemakers" rarely become teachers. At the beginning of each seminar I ask the participants to raise their hands if they were ever thrown out of school, were ever labeled a "difficult student" because of behavior issues, or ever did things in school that they hope their students never discover. To my amazement, on average two or three teachers in a room of one hundred raise their hands.

By the end of the seminar, many teachers tell me that they've begun to understand why it's so difficult to relate to students who have little or no self-control: most of them would never dream of acting the way those students do. In fact, it's very hard for them to *imagine*, let alone understand, what might motivate a child to behave in this manner.

That's not a problem for me! I *was* the student the teachers dreaded—the one who talked too much, never sat still, and defied the adults to make me do anything I didn't want to do. So my "lightbulb moment" as a teacher came when I realized that these were exactly the same issues that I was facing in my own classroom. My experiences as a student gave me the insights I needed to create positive discipline as a teacher.

You know what it means to be a teacher with an out-of-control classroom. You may not know firsthand what it means to be an out-of-control student. It is my wish that my experiences as an educator *and* as a student will give you insight into some of the things that drive children to misbehave and make poor choices.

I hope this book will allow you to change the way you look at children who struggle to function in the classroom. And most important, I hope to provide you with strategies for building the classroom of your dreams: a classroom in which children demonstrate self-control, work well with others, and have optimal learning experiences; a classroom in which you rediscover your love of teaching and are able to share that love with the children whose paths cross yours each year.

How Would You Answer This Question?

Thinking about that goal takes me back to the time when I was just out of college and applying for a teaching job. The very first superintendent who interviewed me raised what I think is a very important question. After a little small talk, she asked, "Can you ever have too much empathy for a child?" I was prepared to respond to every issue on education that you could imagine, but I was suddenly thrown by what seemed to be a very easy question. I got hung up on the word *empathy* and the difference between *empathy* and *sympathy*.

I didn't want to get the question wrong. What was it she wanted to know? Now too much time had passed. I blurted out, "No!" then sat silently waiting for her reaction. She said, "It's important to me that every teacher who works with children in this district be willing to see things from a child's point of view."

She ended the interview shortly after that, and I couldn't help wondering if she had cut things short because I'd given the wrong answer. The drive home was a long one as I wondered what in the world she was trying to learn about me. What did

You need to put yourself in their shoes and do your very best to show understanding.

the question really mean? As soon as I got home, I looked the word up in my *Webster's New World College Dictionary.* This is what I found: "the projection of one's own personality into the personality of another in order to *understand* the person better; ability to *share* in another's emotions, thoughts, or feelings." (The italics are mine.)

Can you go too far in showing another human being that you're trying to see a situation from his point of view? Whether you're right or wrong, agreeing or disagreeing, *understanding* is the key. Children have the right to feel the way they feel. You need to be willing to put yourself in their shoes, acknowledge their feelings, and do your very best to show understanding.

I knew I had answered the question correctly, and I was thrilled when the phone rang the next day and it was the superintendent offering me the position. We have become friends over the years and have talked about that very question with many, many parents and educators. I believe that you can never have too much empathy for a child. I'm glad that she felt that way, too!

2

ACCEPTING WHAT WE CAN'T CHANGE

Empathy is the first key to building a discipline plan for your classroom. The second is acceptance. You know the Serenity Prayer, don't you? It's the one that goes, "God grant me the serenity to accept the things I cannot change; courage to change the things I can; and wisdom to know the difference." I think most of us could use some serenity in the classroom once in a while! So before we start building a discipline plan, let's agree that there are some things we can't change. We just have to accept them for what they are.

What's Past Is Past

We all make mistakes in dealing with children. We all wish we'd said or done something differently at some point. We're not perfect. Somewhere along the line, every single teacher or parent I've met has lost control, overreacted, said something she regrets, or wished she'd done something differently. The best remedies? Take note, reflect, and look for the learning opportunity. Make a commitment to yourself for the next time. And whatever you do, don't beat yourself up. At some time in all of our lives, we did what we had to do to get through the day. Whether we're adults or children, we've all made bad choices. Those choices don't have to define us. This is a life lesson that I hope to share with children: We can't change the past. We *can* make a different choice next time.

School vs. Home

We don't get to decide who they are born to, where they live, or how they are disciplined in their homes. Sometimes that means we don't feel support from home for our efforts to build responsible children who possess self-control. Does that mean our efforts are wasted? Au contraire! I believe that those are the times when we have an awesome opportunity to be ever present in a child's life. A role model who provides positive discipline will remain with a child outside the classroom long after the year ends.

You Can't "Control" Children's Behavior Long Term

Only one person is in your direct control every minute of every day. That person is *you*! You can control how you respond to each situation. My goal is not to control children; it is to facilitate children in controlling themselves. Anytime adults say that they control children, what they're really saying is that they've gained control temporarily. It's always disheartening to hear a teacher say, "They would never do that when they're with me." It shows how superficial the control really is. When children truly learn behaviors, they do not turn those behaviors off and on depending on who's in their presence. We want children to behave well for the right reasons. Those reasons exist even when the children are not in our immediate presence. Our role is to help children learn skills that lead to self-control. Knowing and accepting that is the key to a successful discipline strategy.

It Takes Two to Argue

Do you ever want to be known as a teacher who engages in a power struggle with a five-, six-, or seven-year-old? There can be a fight only if two or more people engage in it. One person must be the one who ends the arguing; often it needs to be the adult. I won't argue with children.

Emotions High = Solutions Low

Many times this simple rule can aid you in a classroom. We often want quick fixes to problems. When a child misbehaves, we want the problem resolved immediately, while the problem is at its height. But often this is the least effective way to go. A child whose emotions are high gets focused on the one and only emotion he currently feels. Maybe Adam is feeling hurt because Zak called him a name. You can try to reprimand Adam for hitting Zak, but every time you try to address the hitting, Adam will retreat to his emotional issue.

In your own life, you've probably had the experience of disagreeing with the way someone handled a situation. Maybe you've thought, "Now's not a good time to address that. I'll talk

One person must be the one who ends the arguing; often it needs to be the adult.

to her later." People (adults as well as children) need time to process things or just to settle down. In those cases, "think time" may be the best response to a behavior problem. It's so hard to think clearly when you're in a heightened emotional state—and if that's true for adults, think how a child must feel! Recognition of this simple fact can save lots of time and energy.

If You Always Do What You Always Do, You'll Always Get What You Always Get

Accept that many of us do what we know. We take our lead either from what was done to us or from what we've learned along the way. Our discipline strategies are no different. We often rely on what we've done before, and if that approach "works," we'll do it again. But sometimes what "works" is only a short-term fix that doesn't resolve the long-term problem. So if you are not satisfied that what you do creates positive long-term changes in thinking and behaviors, maybe it isn't really "working" at all.

If it isn't working, are you willing to try something different? Breaking habits that are long established is challenging for children *and* adults. But I promise that you will reap the benefits by making small changes with the children you teach. Those benefits will fuel your commitment to trying something different.

Every positive thing you do with children is setting the stage for the future.

Of course, change takes commitment. This commitment can give you the power to change your life, to change the lives of your students, and to change education. If your mind and heart tell you it's time for a change, I hope you'll consider some of my suggestions. But first you need to accept one last thing.

Sometimes Your Caring Won't Be Enough

Teaching is a profession filled with caring people who want the best for children. We care deeply and take much of what happens in our classrooms and with "our children" personally. These things touch our hearts. Each of us wants to believe that if we care enough, every child will succeed; every child will learn self-discipline. I would ask you to remember that the children are ours for such a short time, and our caring is sometimes not enough at this stage of their development. If you do all you can and the outcome at the end of a single year doesn't match your hopes, please consider that every positive thing you do with children is setting the stage for the future. You may never see the full results of your actions now, but positive discipline will stay with them long after they leave you.

Please remember, too, that *they* must care. Children must see the value of discipline in their own lives. They must want to learn ways of coping with feelings, getting along with others, and gaining self-control. *We* can care, we can offer alternatives, and we can try to show how those alternatives can create positive changes. But we can't make *them* care. For the plan to work, *they* must care.

As you mull over the things that you cannot change, remember that optimism is a great attribute. Although I accept the things in the present that I can't change, I am ever hopeful that some of what I teach will live on in children. I hope they will treat themselves and others differently because of what they've learned from me. I take joy in believing that even the small things that I do now have the potential to be life changing in the future.

3

What Do We Want & How Do We Get It?

If we're going to create a strong discipline plan, our first step is to identify what the word *discipline* means to us. This is important because our philosophy of discipline will drive our actions, but coming up with a definition is not as easy as it sounds. Every teacher seems to have a slightly different idea of what *discipline* means, because every teacher's background and personal experience are different.

We need help. Let's go back to my *Webster's New World College Dictionary,* which defines discipline this way: "training that develops self-control, character, or orderliness and efficiency." That's the first definition. The second definition is "strict control to enforce obedience."

Go back and read those definitions again. The second one suggests that someone else is exercising control that results in obedience. The first refers to the teaching of *self*-control. It's important to understand that my ultimate goal for any aspect of discipline is based on the first definition. So I will state again that my goal always is *positive* discipline, with a focus on helping children *to control themselves.*

Many of us have dealt with the child who seemingly can't be controlled. We threaten, we bribe, we beg, we scream, all to no avail. The child's behavior and motivations seem alien to us, and we just don't "get" what's driving him. All we know is that it sure isn't us! Nothing we do works to control this child.

Think about that. *Nothing we do works to control this child.* But remember, that wasn't the goal. The goal wasn't for us to be the ones making it work, and the goal wasn't for us to control the child. The irony is that the key to a positive discipline plan is finding a way to drive every child's behavior and motivation for learning through those mysterious forces that are *inside him.*

Every teacher's goal should be to make sure that each child's emotions and actions are driven by the person to whom they matter the most: the child. We want children to work and behave, but we want them to do those things for reasons that mean something to them. The ultimate goal is for the teacher to play a smaller and smaller role each time the child faces a challenge in terms of behavior—and eventually for the child to find his internal control and take the lead himself.

No One Plans to Fail, but We Often Fail to Plan

It's all well and good to have goals, but how do we make the time to meet them? All teachers know how much time it takes to plan and set up a new classroom. There's so much to do to get ready for the children. Then we have to pay atten-

You might say that some children already know how to behave. That's true. Some children come to us knowing how to read and write, too.

tion to the curriculum requirements and the standards for each grade level in reading, writing, math, science, social studies, and more. We research, plot, and prepare the approaches we'll use to teach each subject and meet each standard. But how well do we research, plot, and prepare the discipline plan that we'll put forth in our classrooms? When it comes to discipline, do we set the standards, allow for differentiation, and know our goals? Do we know how we'll assess success and, more important, how we'll address failure? I believe that each teacher must set the goals for her classroom, choose and implement a discipline plan, and then decide whether the plan is working and the goals are being reached.

Our first priority has to be to decide what the standards for discipline are and what the curriculum for teaching those standards will be. Now, you might say that some children already know how to be kind and how to behave. That's true. Some children come to us knowing how to read and write, too. But not everyone. So we must establish our standards for discipline and our plan for teaching them. We also must be willing to assess whatever discipline plan we already have in place and determine whether it's working. If it's not, we must be open to changing the current plan and to developing a new one. In the end, we'll need a toolbox of management techniques to make certain that every child can succeed. But that will come later. First, as with all good lessons, we need to have a plan. To create that plan, we need to know what works.

What Works

Research has shown that the discipline plans of effective schools have certain characteristics in common. Let's take a look at some of those characteristics, and let's think about how we can apply them. Are you ready?

A Constant Focus on Learning

In effective schools, the focus is on learning, not on correcting behavior issues in the short term. So the discipline plans in these schools have long-term goals, and both staff and students understand how important those goals are. Effective schools monitor progress in meeting behavior goals just as they monitor progress in meeting other learning goals, and they adjust their discipline plans if they need to, just as they adjust other plans.

In these schools, teachers recognize that children who don't have self-control need to be taught what it is and how to achieve it. When children come to school and can't read, we teach them to read. When children come to school and can't write, we teach them to write. If they don't understand math, we explain and teach them math. When they come to school and don't behave, do we chastise them? No, we *teach* them to behave.

High Expectations + Clear Rules

In effective schools, teachers take time to establish the rules with the students. Students understand why the rules exist and how important they are to all members of the community. It's understood that each child is capable of following the rules, and it's expected that each child will follow them. We will never truly know what a child is capable of doing unless we expect the best. Children need to know that we have high expectations and that everyone must put his best foot forward. And if they try but don't reach the ultimate goal? They need to know that as long as they are striving to do their best, that's acceptable.

They also need to clearly understand what the rules are. Sometimes children question the rules because we have taught them to question rules. When we say yes, we should mean yes, and when we say no, we should mean no. Saying yes or no and then wavering on that response teaches children to argue with you until you change your mind. We must be prepared to stick with our original answer. If a child catches you off guard and you're not sure, say so. When you respond with "I need time to think about that before I answer," you teach children to think things through.

Acting vs. Reacting

In an effective school, faculty members establish proactive strategies for creating a thriving learning environment. They think about "what could happen," and they develop strategies for dealing with certain types of situations before those situations come up. If we anticipate what might happen and know what we'll do when it does, we can keep the focus on learning and avoid getting distracted by the issue at hand. Effective schools build a sense of community, teach communication skills, and demonstrate that they hold internal motivation and self-control in high esteem.

A Positive Atmosphere & Strong Role Models

Effective schools put the spotlight on positive behavior; they don't concentrate on the negative. Teachers present discipline in positive terms. They teach that misbehavior is an opportunity to learn and that new chances for success exist. They offer constant support for children in solving problems. They model problem-

Effective schools teach children to become problem solvers.

solving skills and teach them in real-world situations. The adults set a good example by talking about the choices they make and by pointing out that in most instances, we all have control over those choices.

A Problem-Solving Philosophy

Effective schools recognize that students must learn how to deal with their own thoughts and emotions. So they teach children to become problem solvers. Punishments and rewards exist in these schools, but they are not the focus. Instead, the emphasis is on helping children to learn what their choices are and how those choices affect their lives.

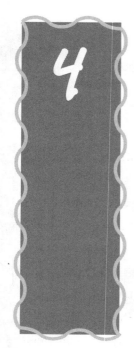

4

WHAT HAVE WE TRIED?

Now that we've seen what works in building positive discipline plans, let's take a look at some of the other things that have been tried in schools across America—and why some of those things *haven't* worked. Let's also look at some things that, even if they do work, may not be so great for long-term learning.

Most of these approaches are some version of either threatening or bribing. The problem with threatening and bribing is that over time, they lead children to believe that somebody or something else governs their choices and is responsible for the things they do. Now, I am the first to admit that sometimes threatening or bribing a child is the quickest and most effective way to gain control, and so I have certainly done both. But if teaching *self*-control is my goal, threatening and bribing should not become the focus of my discipline plan.

Why not? Versions of threatening and bribing plans have been in place in schools for years. Let's look at some that may sound familiar.

Threats

In behavior plans based on threats, the teacher uses her voice, status, size, or ability to provide or take away to threaten her students. The threat is that "you'll do what I want . . . or else!" There must be a fear factor involved.

Sometimes this type of plan works. Other times threats seem to bring out the worst in children. Our brains are wired to make us instinctively try either to get away from things that threaten us (that's the "flight" response) or to take the opposite approach and attack (that's the "fight" response). I think that's why for some children, ultimatums are invitations to defiance. Think about how often an ultimatum invites rebelliousness.

Let's look at discipline plans based on threats.

Pull a Card

This discipline system is one of the most popular ones I've found in the many schools I've visited. I employed it myself for several years. In this system, the teacher has a pocket chart. Each child's name appears above one pocket, and each pocket has a number of cards in it. In my experience, the cards are usually blank and color coded. For example, each child might have four cards—one green, one blue, one yellow, and one red. Some teachers use fewer cards; some use more.

The pocket chart is prominently displayed in the classroom, and everybody knows what the colors mean. Each child's cards start out in a certain order; the goal is to keep your cards in the

The system works well only for children who must _occasionally_ pull a card.

original order for the entire day. Usually the policy is that if you break a rule or behave inappropriately, you must "pull a card" and go down a level in the color scheme. Let's say that at the beginning of the day the red card is at the back, with yellow, blue, and green in front of it in that order. The green card is the one you want to keep in the front. Now let's say that the colors denote the following:

- Green: Excellent day
- Blue: Warning #1
- Yellow: Warning #2
- Red: Note or phone call home ("bad day")

Each time the child is asked to "pull a card," we assume she knows that she's not following the rules and is now being given a chance to keep the cards from going down another level. The teacher keeps some kind of tally, and at the end of the day or week, he sends the tally home. This tells the child's parents how many times she pulled cards and what color she ended up with. This system is supposed to show children and parents what kind of week it was for each child.

There are a couple of problems that appear to plague this system. The most obvious is that the same children are always the ones pulling the cards. When I talk to teachers about the system, they report that it works well only for children who must _occasionally_ pull a card. I wonder if these children really warrant such a system. Teachers also report that the children who end up with the red card on Monday are most often the same ones who end up with red on Tuesday and Wednesday and. . . . You get the idea. So we must ask ourselves, "Is this working?"

Let me share with you a real, live version of this system at work. I am assigned to teach an inclusion classroom with very high-needs students. The children's behaviors range from excellent to spitting, biting, and running. In this school, "pull a card" is the school-wide system. Therefore, it's not only the classroom teacher who has the authority to tell children to pull a card; any teacher or staff member who witnesses or experiences a problem can insist that a child pull a card. The problem can be with the child's attitude, behavior, or work.

One day the children in my class go off to lunch. During lunch there are a few "episodes," and pretty soon the lunch lady is running out of patience. By the time I arrive to pick up the children at the end of lunch period, things are out of control.

The first thing I see is a sobbing child in a heap on the floor. In this instance, it happens to be the child we all dream of having in our class. She is a wonderful student and is kind and polite. On top of that, she always has two sharpened pencils, and you have never, ever seen her at the pencil sharpener. She is your dream student. I rush to her to ask, "What's wrong?" Before she can answer, the lunch lady screams, "She spilled her milk everywhere today! She needs to pull a card!"

As she screams, my little sweetheart of a student is whispering, "It was an accident. I've never had to pull a card. My mom will be so disappointed. I'm so sorry; it just tipped over." The child is a complete wreck. She has never had anything but a green card and is absolutely destroyed by this situation. I doubt she'll make it through the day. I whisper in her ear, "Don't worry, hon. Mrs. Whyte won't make you pull a card. I know it was an accident." This is a child whose conscience and sense of right and wrong are in no way dictated by those cards. She feels terrible about the incident, and in my mind that's punishment enough.

Now my attention is drawn to the second student the lunch lady has started to scream about. This is one of my boys. He has very little to no self-control. He is smiling as the lunch lady tells me that he must pull two cards today. He tells the classmate behind him that he doesn't even have two left! He then turns to the classmate who's on the floor sobbing and says, "I have to pull two. It's no big deal. Usually I don't have any more cards anyway! Sometimes Mrs. Whyte gives me more colored cards. I think I need more chances."

He turns to me and calls, "Can I get more cards?" He remembers that there have been times when I've added cards in other colors (orange, purple, pink, black, maroon, indigo . . .) because he is a child who struggles and needs more chances. The lunch lady looks at me with disgust. I try to ignore the child and the worker and to get the children out of the cafeteria as quickly as possible.

Is this system working for either child? Does it teach them the rewards and consequences of the choices they make? Will it teach them to exercise self-control? Does it allow for occasional slipups or accidents? Does it encourage learning that will result in a positive change for the future?

One of my biggest concerns is for the child whose card is red every day by lunchtime. What is his motivation to change his behavior this day? It's already been labeled a "bad day." Aren't there times when he might think, "What else can this teacher do?" Simply labeling it a "bad day" may make it become a bad day. I can certainly say that this system has ruined more than one of mine!

It's scary how often children will "live to a label," becoming whatever they're accused of being.

Public Humiliation

This is another form of threatening children. We announce to others that "Joe is ruining it for all of us, and if he doesn't stop misbehaving, we will collectively be upset. He is rude." We might add, "It's his fault that we can't complete this activity." Think about this type of statement and what it says to the child. First, it says he should stop his behavior because it's important to *us*! Where is the importance to *him*? Second, it tells him that we as teachers have the power to make others mad at him or, worse, not like him anymore. And it suggests that they won't like him because what he's doing defines who he is. Actions do *not* define children. Anytime our language insinuates that they do, it hurts children's ability to believe that they can change. It's scary how often children will "live to a label," becoming whatever awful thing they're accused of being.

"Go to the Office" & Other Removal Strategies

At those times when we resort to these strategies to keep ourselves sane, their use may be warranted. If you're at the end of your rope, I highly recommend separating yourself from the child (see "The Toolbox of Management Techniques," page 157). But this should not be the first line of defense. Sending a child to the office or some other place is another action that's based on the teacher's having the power.

I'm a firm believer in "think time," which may require removal, but that's not what I'm talking about here. What I'm talking about here are those times when we're angry and frustrated and we want to punish the child, so we ask her to leave the classroom. But that's it; we don't intervene in any other way. We don't guide the child to correct her behavior; we just get her out of the classroom.

The hitch is that many times children see this approach as bullying on the part of the teacher. Instead of solving the problem, it can lead to resentment. And resentment tends to escalate the problem instead of solving it.

Perception Is Everything

With any of the plans I've just described, we're threatening students with some form of punishment. But we need to realize that for many children, punishment doesn't necessarily lead to better behavior. Instead, it can provoke the following reactions:

- A perceived need for revenge
- The fight-or-flight instinct
- A feeling of helplessness
- A belief that others control him

Bribes

In behavior plans based on bribes, the teacher offers a tangible reward for good behavior. As with plans based on threats, many children view these plans as something controlled by the teacher. Consider these examples.

The One-Size-Fits-All Pizza Plan

When I was a first-year teacher, a more experienced teacher told me her secret for dealing with behavior issues: write the word *PIZZA* on the board in big, bold letters. Why hadn't I

By 10:30, as I frantically explained that "you only have a quarter of the _A_ left," I had a feeling this "pizza plan" wasn't going to work.

thought of that? All I needed to do, the teacher assured me, was to explain to the children that each day, their goal would be to try to keep the letters of that word on the board by behaving and doing their work. If anyone broke any of the class rules, I would erase one of the letters. Each morning we would assess the number of letters left on the board. The goal would be to have at least one letter left on Friday. The reward was that if the class succeeded in keeping any or all of the letters on the board, I would buy them pizza.

I tried it out first thing on Monday morning. I carefully explained the plan to the children. I fielded their questions and felt comfortable that they understood the reward and how to earn it. I was quite sure that they were motivated to earn the pizza. By 9:00 a.m., we had firmly established our plan, and I wrote the letters on the board. By 10:30, as I frantically explained to the children that "you only have a quarter of the _A_ left," I had a feeling this "pizza plan" wasn't going to work. And you know what's the hardest thing for me to admit? Not only did I try a version of this again the next week, but I tried it many more times in different classrooms later on. And it _never_ worked very well!

Maybe I should have noticed the red flag when the other teacher was explaining this system to me. When I asked whether it tended to get expensive, she replied, "Not to worry—they don't earn it very often." I don't know about you, but I'm thinking maybe I should have stopped right there!

When was the last time you expected the employee at the grocery store to hand you a lollipop and thank you for not stealing today?

It sounded like a good idea at the time, but looking back, I have a lot more questions. These are some of the things I wonder:

1. If the reward is for the whole group, is it necessarily appealing to all of the children in the group?
2. Is it ever good to use food as a reward?
3. If you're going to use a reward system with young children, it's usually most effective when the reward comes right on the heels of the action it's rewarding. For some children, five days might just as well be five years. Is that an effective system?
4. Is it fair that a child who follows the rules all week loses the reward because some of his classmates misbehave?
5. What is this teaching children that will help them to learn self-control?

Stickers, Candy & Prizes

Teachers have spent their own children's college funds on these strategies. There are many versions, but they all boil down to this: "Do what I want, and I will give you something in return." These strategies scare me the most. I worry that we're creating children who expect repeated and often excessive reinforcement simply for doing what's right. What happened to doing what's right because it's the right thing to do? When was the last time you expected the employee at the grocery store to stop you on the way out, hand you a lollipop, and thank you for not stealing today?

When we use these prize strategies, we're not preparing children for the real world—a world that holds many rewards and consequences, both tangible and intangible. Do any of us really believe that a sticker, a piece of candy, or a plastic parachute man will teach children to have self-control and do what is right? And isn't that what we really want?

Many researchers have studied the effects of extrinsic rewards on intrinsic motivation. A 1999 review of these studies found that external, tangible rewards significantly *reduce* a child's internal motivation. Isn't that just the opposite of what we're trying to accomplish?

Never let it be said that I didn't offer a huge prize to the children I taught. Sometimes other teachers (remedial reading, gym, and so on) would give my students prizes. Whenever that happened, the children would come back to my classroom and ask why I didn't give prizes. I always told them that they had the best prize of all: me! I would tell them that they had a teacher who cared about them and created a fun, exciting place to learn, and that was truly a prize!

I have rewarded children with tangible things, but most often I follow this basic philosophy: I reward good choices with words and deeds, and I respond to bad choices by redirecting the child. Each of the plans I've described lacks one key element: a chance for children to learn from the choices they make. We can do better than that.

5

TIME TO GET STARTED!

It's easy to identify what doesn't work. It's harder to figure out what does. In this book, I want to give you a discipline strategy based on teaching children to control themselves. It is my hope that this will offer you a new way to think about the discipline plan in your classroom and maybe some ways to modify it to allow children to learn from the mistakes they make. I firmly believe that second (and third and fourth . . .) chances, with guidance, can change a child's life.

To create that kind of plan, we need to prioritize. What do we most want and expect from students in terms of behavior, attitude, and work? Once we have defined those goals, we can lead the students in identifying what rules the classroom needs in order to function smoothly. Discuss why the rules are important, as well as what would happen if they were not followed. Post the rules in the classroom. Remind the children that, working together, they created this list. Be sure to communicate this in a positive manner. Emphasize that they have the power to make choices and can control their future.

Building a positive discipline plan requires a firm foundation. I believe that the strongest foundation has four important cornerstones.

Cornerstone #1: Self-control. The ability of each person to manage his own behavior and communication. We need to forget about trying to control children and instead support them in controlling themselves.

Cornerstone #2: Choice. The potential for selecting good or bad alternatives in every situation. We need to communicate to children that we each determine much of what happens in our lives by the choices we make. We also want them to recognize that their choices often affect other people.

Cornerstone #3: Communication. The way in which we convey our needs, wants, and opinions through both words and actions. We must teach children to communicate in positive ways and to keep the lines of communication open.

Cornerstone #4: Community. A sense of belonging to a group or groups, such as family, friends, neighborhood, and school. Communities play a vital role in our lives. If we can help students to understand what it means to be part of the school community, they can get a better sense of what it means to belong to the many other communities in their lives.

The following chapters describe each of these cornerstones in much more detail. I hope they will give you lots of ideas for building a positive discipline plan that will support your classroom goals.

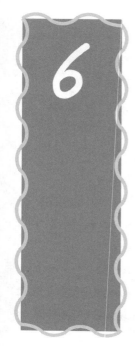

CORNERSTONE #1: SELF-CONTROL

Self-control is the heart and soul of the discipline plan. We want our students to become productive, conscientious learners and citizens. We need to teach them that there are rules and boundaries, that choices have rewards and consequences, and that in many situations, students have the power to determine their own thoughts, attitudes, and behaviors. Children who are motivated by something within themselves take responsibility for their emotions and actions in every aspect of their lives. These are important concepts. They can also be complicated, and we need to break them down so that children can understand them. Here are some things to think about.

Different Situations Call for Different Behaviors

At times children have a difficult time making the transition from one situation to another and appear not to demonstrate self-control. Think of times when you've been on the playground on a beautiful day. The children are running, playing, laughing, and exploring space. Then you go inside, and they can't seem to settle down. The exact behaviors that were appropriate on the playground are inappropriate in the classroom.

Inside, we tell children to walk (no running), to do their work (no more playtime), to be serious (no laughing), and to sit in their seats (no exploring space). It takes self-control to use different behaviors in different situations.

Children can learn that behavior that's appropriate in one place is not appropriate in a different place. Ask, "Do you act differently in church than you do at the zoo?" Write the names of places (the grocery store, the playground, the classroom, the soccer field, inside a car, on the bus, and so on) on individual index cards and have each pair or group of students randomly take a card. Ask them to list behaviors that are appropriate in the location that's listed on the card.

Once each pair or group has completed their list, ask the groups to trade

WHERE AM I?

Before you ask students to list behaviors that are appropriate in specific places, try giving clues such as these and asking them to guess where those behaviors would be appropriate. Ask which statements helped them to figure out that you're talking about the shopping mall.

In this place:

- There is a lot of space, but you need to walk.

- No skateboards are allowed.

- If you take it off the rack and then you decide not to buy it, you have to hang it back up.

- When you are ready to make a purchase, you stand in line and wait your turn.

Children have a hard time understanding that we truly need very few things in life, and that the list of needs doesn't include iPods.

lists. Do the same behaviors apply to the other group's location? Why are they acceptable or not acceptable?

Wants vs. Needs

Self-control also entails understanding wants versus needs. Often children believe that they need something when really they just want it. At times, it's very difficult for young children to understand that we can't always get what we want. Explaining and modeling the distinction between wanting and needing is a valuable life lesson, and you can find many opportunities for teaching it in the classroom. What if there are twelve vanilla cupcakes and twelve chocolate, but fourteen children want the chocolate? What if all the red paper is gone and that's the color you wanted? What are your choices in these situations? If we teach children what they can do at times like these, they'll be better prepared to transfer those lessons to the bigger issues in life.

I ask students to write in their journals about things they need. Then I respond with a personal message in each journal. It's heartwarming when children say they need family and pets but disheartening when they list things such as bikes, iPods, and candy. Children have a hard time understanding that we truly need very few things in life, and that although the list of needs includes air, water, food, sleep, and shelter, it doesn't include iPods.

Why Does It Take So Long?

Patience is a form of self-control. Adults are often not good at waiting. Why are we surprised when children have such a hard time? Sometimes when we say to a child, "Wait five minutes," we might as well say, "Wait your whole life." Children need to be taught the concept of time, and we can do some simple things to begin that process.

For example, use a timer to show how long it should take to complete a specific task, such as sharpening a pencil. How often this simple act creates a riot in the classroom! You know the child who takes too long. Or the one who consistently sharpens her pencil to such a point that the minute the lead hits the paper, it breaks. Or the child who never stops sharpening his pencils. (That's the one who has a dozen pencils that are about an inch long.) Demonstrate how long this process should take, then have the students follow suit.

Then figure out together how long it should take someone to wash his hands, choose a book, or put on her coat. Ask the children to tell you about something that takes a lot of time and something that lasts only a second. Talking about time helps children learn to manage it better.

Following Directions

Self-control is often displayed in a child's ability to follow directions. When we tell children to follow our directions, we

assume they know how to do that. When they don't, it's frustrating for both the teacher and the child. Think of a time when you were cooking, adding the ingredients for a recipe one at a time. Did you double-check (maybe triple-check) to be sure you were putting in the right amounts? Did you reread the recipe several times to make sure that you'd put everything you needed into the bowl? When was the last time you read an unfamiliar recipe, followed it, and produced a batch of cookies without checking the cookbook once?

Following directions is a learned skill. I tell children that I always list the dry ingredients from the recipe in my head, so that I can go to the pantry and retrieve all of them at once. Then I look at the list of wet ingredients and try to remember all of them. Lots of times I have to go back and check. I could get frustrated or just tell myself, "I won't check; I'll take my chances," but those aren't the best choices for the situation. When you learn strategies for following directions, you learn a piece of self-discipline, and that's the reason it's good to give students activities that let them practice such an important skill.

When children play Simon Says or follow the motions associated with a song, they learn to stay on task, but sometimes children need more support than that. Teachers often say that young children don't follow directions. When that's the case, it might be appropriate to examine how many directions you're giving to a child at one time. Think how hard it would be to remember all the ingredients in a complicated recipe! If a child has a hard time holding all the directions in her short- or long-term memory, maybe she needs a backup plan for recalling the directions and their order.

Other Occasions That Call for Self-Control

Other things require self-control, too. Children must know how to manage time and space, how to develop a plan, and how to follow through on commitments. And self-control includes self-restraint. Children need to understand the concepts of personal space and shared space. They need to learn that keeping their hands and feet (teeth, too!) to themselves is important. All of those things show self-control. We need to teach each skill, model it, and give children opportunities to practice it.

Keep in mind that children need to practice not only the physical part of self-restraint but also the emotional part. Many issues of self-control involve emotions and words, so being in command of our language is as important as being in command of our behavior.

Building & Understanding Self-Control

Self-control is a difficult concept for many young children to grasp. In their homes, adults make many decisions for children and often run to their aid in times of stress. Now the little ones find themselves in classrooms with so many other children who have needs of their own. It's time to learn that each of us must take responsibility for what happens in our own lives.

Agreeing to Disagree

Do we all have to think alike? It's valuable for children to learn that each of us hears and interprets things in a unique way, according to our abilities and past experiences. There are times when you look at something one way and someone else sees the same thing in a different way. It's okay to agree to disagree. In class discussions, ask children what they think or feel about a character in a book they've been reading. Make sure to ask why they think or feel that way and then reiterate that each of us can have a different opinion. Trouble begins when we believe that everyone needs to think the same way we do.

Immediate Satisfaction

We are born with the instinct to demand whatever we need. Babies cry to signal that they're hungry, restless, or need their diapers changed. Later, everybody wants what he wants, and he wants it *now*! Not getting that immediate satisfaction is a tough notion for children to grasp. You can help by providing opportunities to talk about and role-play getting what we want when we want it.

It's also important to illustrate that there are times when we can get immediate satisfaction but it costs us in the long run. Have you ever heard that saying "It was worth the wait"? What kinds of things do adults and children need to wait for? I like to tell children that even when I want a new piece of clothing, I won't buy it if it isn't on sale. Every time I've ever bought an

item of clothing at full price, I've seen it go on sale a week or so later. I achieved immediate satisfaction by buying it at the time, but I've always wished I'd waited and saved some money. I would have had the same piece of clothing and more money.

Does "No" Mean "Maybe"?

I worry a great deal that adults have trained children to expect that "no" can be changed to "yes" with enough badgering. So often I've heard parents say no, sometimes even saying it several times, and then I've seen them give the child what he wanted. For example, here's an incident I witnessed in a grocery store. A boy picked up a candy bar and asked his mom, "May I have this?" Her response was, "No, I'm not buying that today." He said, "Please." She said, "Not today. I just bought you the fruit roll-ups you wanted. I'm not buying candy." The little boy whined. "Please, Mom," he said. "This is my favorite candy bar, and I haven't seen it in a lot of stores." Mom's turn: "I said no, and by the way, that candy bar is in every store." In a last-ditch attempt, the boy mustered his very saddest look and said, "But, Mom, you got Tommy [I take it Tommy was his brother] a candy bar last time *he* helped you do the grocery shopping." The mom caved! She said, "Okay, but I'm not buying anything else, so get in line."

What's the lesson in this scenario? Badger me until I do what you want. Continue the pleading and continue the whining until

They could scream, cry, ask again at a different time, or volunteer at the local animal clinic.

I cave. Children learn very quickly to find the gray area between the black and the white. When you allow them to do that, you encourage more of the same behavior. What they learn is not to believe you when you finally do want "no" to mean "no."

That's not the lesson you want to teach. Instead, "no" means "no," "yes" means "yes," and if you're not sure, you should say, "Let me think for a minute before I answer." Don't blame children if they've learned to badger. You can learn to badger only if someone allows you to, and you'll continue only if it works for you. We seldom continue to use strategies that don't work in our lives. Badgering is a learned behavior that can be unlearned.

What Happens When You Can't Get What You Want?

Sometimes we must wait to do or have something we want. Sometimes we can't do or have it at all. What do we do when we can't have it? Ask your students how many of them would like to have a puppy or a kitten. Ask them how many of their parents don't want them to have one. If they want a puppy or a kitten and Mom and Dad say no, what are their choices?

Let children brainstorm things that they could do. Maybe they could scream, cry, ask again at a different time, write a letter explaining why they should get a pet, accept that they can't have one, or become a pet sitter or a volunteer at the local animal clinic. Illustrate that life goes on when we don't get what we want.

Following Through on Commitments

A friend invites you to spend the night. You say yes, but then you have an opportunity to go to another friend's house, and you think that would be more fun. What do you do? The answer should be easy: you follow through on the commitment you've made. Children need to know how important it is to do what we say we will and "honor our word." Many of us heard this from our parents or grandparents when we were growing up, but it seems that too many of our little ones think it's okay to renege on a commitment. Teach children to stand by the commitments they make. If we commit to someone or something, we need to follow through. This shows self-control.

A classroom scenario for teaching this concept might include choosing a partner for a small project with the understanding that each pair must stay committed to each other to get the job done. Make sure students know that switching to a different partner is not an option.

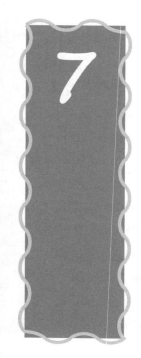

CORNERSTONE #2: CHOICE

We all make choices in life. Some are good, and some are bad. Some empower us, and some hurt others. The truth is that we make hundreds of choices each day without much thought at all. We choose whether or not to hit the snooze button, which side of the bed we'll get up from, how hot the shower will be, how long we'll brush our teeth, what we'll have for breakfast, and when we'll leave for work.

Common sense tells me that there are often constraints on my choices. Maybe I forgot to set the alarm, so I don't have the option of hitting the snooze button. Perhaps my husband is sleeping on the side of the bed I want to get up from, and you may know that saying, "Don't poke a bear." There could be no hot water for my shower, and I might have left my toothbrush at my sister's house when I visited. That would limit my time in the shower and prevent me from brushing my teeth. There most definitely are limited choices for breakfast at my house. And if I'm going to be at school on time, I may not have a huge choice in what time I leave the house.

What if I didn't let these constraints get in my way? What if I decided to get up when my eyes opened every day? What if I just poked the bear and got up from that side of the bed? What if I skipped the shower and the toothbrushing? What if I ate breakfast at the diner every day, with a menu full of choices? And what if I decided which days I would go to work and what time I would arrive? Ooh, life would be interesting!

We all make choices. Some are easy; some are hard. Some force us to weigh many pros and cons, and some we make without any thought. Then we live with the rewards and consequences of the choices we've made. Let's teach our students to make choices and to live with the rewards and consequences of their choices. Let's teach them to understand that they ultimately hold the power to make better choices and that each new day brings new opportunities to make different choices.

Good vs. Bad Choices

We must teach children that we all have the power to make choices in our lives. Some choices affect only us, but many also affect the people around us. When children make good choices in our classrooms, they will be able to continue to make choices. When they make bad choices, they will be offered opportunities to learn from them and make better choices in the future.

If children consistently make bad choices, it may be necessary for you to temporarily make their choices for them. Ultimately, you are responsible for the safety of the class and may need to make choices for a child who endangers another child or who constantly impedes another's ability to learn. But that should be the exception. The norm should be for you to model, guide, and assist the child in making good choices. If we always tell children what to do and how long to do it, how will they become independent learners who understand how to make choices?

The objective should be to emphasize choice in every aspect of the school day. Children learn to make good choices when they're responsible for their choices and when they feel capable of self-determination.

The Rewards & Consequences of Choices

One of the most effective ways to show that we all make choices that result in rewards and consequences is to model this for students. Even teachers make choices—good and bad. We go to bed too late, we don't always get our work finished on time, and most of us choose to eat things that aren't good for us. The great majority of us have overreacted to situations and have done or said things that we regret. We struggle with choices every day. Children need to know that!

One simple way to illustrate good versus bad choices is to tell children about a few of the choices you've made. Remember to include both the good and the bad. In addition, model good choices within your classroom. Use manners, treat others as you would want to be treated, acknowledge emotions, and don't do anything you wouldn't want a child to imitate. Talk out your choices as you make each one. Speak often of the good feelings you get when you choose to do nice things for others. Talk about how the good choice of being kind, for example, has many

My plan doesn't quite work out because I sit down on the couch and fall asleep.

rewards: it makes you feel good, and it makes people want to be around you, so you have friends.

One of the good choices you want to encourage is the choice to follow directions, so remind children of the rewards associated with making that choice. When they complete their work without your having to repeat the directions, they gain valuable time. Be sure that they see this reward: let them benefit from the time gained when they are on target. Offer children opportunities to play a game, read a magazine, or complete some other engaging task when their work is complete. Tell them that we all like to do something fun once we've finished our work. Talk to them about what you like to do in your spare time and how they can gain more time for fun by staying on task and being focused.

A more structured lesson on choice might look like this:

I take a piece of chart paper and write *Friday, Saturday, Sunday,* and *Monday* down the left side. I tell the children that I would like to show them that even I make choices, both good and bad. "For example," I might say, "I like to plan to get my work done on Friday after school so that I'm ready for all of you on Monday. That's my responsibility. It's a good plan, and I want to follow through. The problem is that by Friday afternoon when you've all left, I think, 'Oh, shucks. I should just go home.' So I pack up my teacher bag and head home."

I tell the children that my plan at that point is to get the work done at home on Friday night, but it doesn't quite work out because I sit down on the couch and fall asleep. That's a good

I want to get my work done, but think about it: a free dinner! Excellent choice.

choice when you're tired but a bad choice if you need to get work done.

Not to worry. Although I need to cross out Friday (and I do that on the chart paper), I still have Saturday and Sunday to get the work done. "I decide that's okay," I tell the children. "After all, I won't see you until Monday. So on Saturday I get up and think, 'I should get that work done early.' But Mr. Whyte wants me to go to the soccer game. I decide the work can wait, and off to soccer we go. What a great choice, as it is a warm, sunny day and my favorite team wins! Then Mr. Whyte offers to buy me dinner. Now who would refuse a free dinner? I want to get my work done, but think about it: a free dinner! Excellent choice. I'm full and I didn't even have to pay. Saturday slips away, and I still haven't done my work.

"I must now cross out Saturday," I explain to the children, "as I've made many choices, but not the one to get my work done. Once again, there's time—I still have Sunday to get ready for my little Smarties on Monday. I wake up on Sunday ready to work, but my mom comes by and wants to have coffee. I love my mom and I love coffee, so guess what I choose? Yes, I spend time with my mom and drink one of my favorite beverages. But I don't get my work done.

"Sunday night comes. Mr. Whyte goes to bed, my children go to bed, and I am oh so tired. But I am out of choices.

"I have wonderful excuses for what's brought me here. Who wouldn't go home early, who doesn't like to have someone buy her dinner, and who doesn't like to spend time with her mom? The bottom line is that I made choices, and now it's my responsibility to do what needs to be done to follow through on the commitment that I have to all of you! It is *my responsibility*."

I tell the children that this is exactly what I expect from them. I expect them to be responsible for their choices. I want them to know that some choices will have good outcomes and some choices will have bad outcomes, but the choices are *ours*, and we must live with them.

I explain that I must stay up late Sunday night to get ready for school on Monday. It's the right thing to do. Next time, I might make different choices.

The saying "Actions speak louder than words" seems so appropriate. If we model the process of making choices and explain the corresponding outcomes, children will come to understand the role that self-determination plays in our lives. Showing by example is one of the most powerful tools parents and teachers have for promoting self-control. We need to explain

the process of making good choices, model it, and live it. In turn, we hope that children will make good choices, too. The objective is for each child's good choices to be motivated by internal forces.

Choice Builds Responsibility

Providing even the smallest choices can build responsibility in children. As teachers, our role has sometimes been defined as "boss of the class." But whose boss are we really? When it comes right down to it, we can boss only ourselves. We can't control others. We can't make children read, make them kind, or make them behave. We must help them to learn that reading is a good choice, a lifelong skill that opens doors. We must lead them to see that being kind has its rewards. People are often kind in return, and most of us get satisfaction from how people react to our kindness.

We can't make children behave either, but we can help them to see the outcomes of inappropriate behavior. It's easy to say, "You bite, so move your desk," but maybe there's a better way. Could we point out the consequence of the bad choice by saying, "Biting hurts, and other children don't like to sit next to someone who bites, so please move your desk"? We sure could!

We can help children to understand that most of the time, there are alternative choices, and most important, they hold the power to make their own choices. Self-control can be learned, and it can be nurtured in most children through the teaching and modeling of choices. Talking with the biter at a later time, you can reiterate why children don't like to sit or play with children who bite. You can ask why the child bit someone and what she thinks she could have done instead. You can ensure that she

To provide choices, you must be willing to let go of some control.

doesn't have the opportunity to bite another child. But you can't control her actions, so you can't make her stop biting.

To provide choices, you must be willing to let go of some control. You must believe that the long-term gain is worth the time and energy spent helping children learn to make better decisions. Most of all, you need to acknowledge that children will learn responsibility as they learn to make their own choices.

Be Proactive in Identifying Choices

A proactive stance is based on establishing rules and ensuring that children know them. If you have done this, then before going to the carpet for Morning Meeting you might speak with a child who bites. Remind the child of the rules (we keep our hands, feet, and other body parts to ourselves). Explain to her that you remember how she felt too crowded on the carpet the last time, so she bit her neighbor in frustration. Remind the child that it is often crowded on the carpet because children like to be close to the book or chart that you're using. Then remind her that if someone should get too close to her, she has choices: she can move over if space allows, she can use a kind voice to ask the other child to move over, or she can ask you if she may return to her desk. Be sure to remind her that biting another child is *not* an acceptable choice.

A Way out of a Bad Choice

Even if a child is already making a poor choice, is there a way out? A gift we can give to children is to identify those times when there are better choices available than the one they're currently making or considering making.

That's an improvement over the alternative. Often when children make bad choices, teachers issue ultimatums. The truth is that many times ultimatums invite noncompliance, and many times they lead to power struggles. When a child in your class makes a bad choice, remember that you want the child to be responsible and to make a better choice. You also want to resolve the situation and get the entire class where they need to be. Anytime a child can make a better choice and the class can continue on, it's a win-win situation.

Let's examine a situation in which a child's bad choice can really be a learning opportunity. Although you know that some

situations call for "think time," let's assume this is an instance in which you feel you can address the issue on the spot. Say that a child crawls under a desk and hangs on to the leg when you say it's time to go to music. This is a bad choice, but the choice has been made. You could give an ultimatum—"Get out from under that desk now!" But chances are that a child who's behaving like this is not open to demands. He may stay put; he may yell back; he might even spit if you get too close.

The goal is to get the child to recognize the bad choice and make a different one. You need to state the facts in a matter-of-fact voice: "I

know you don't like to leave the class [acknowledge the feeling], but we've talked about appropriate responses to this. This is not one of them. You're under the desk, we need to go to music, and what you're doing is not a good choice. You can either get out from under the desk by yourself and get in line, or you can take my hand and I'll walk you to the line. Which would you prefer? Please make your choice now." Be sure to emphasize the issue of control: "You decide."

This tells the child that his feelings have been accepted, and it offers a win-win alternative: the child gets an acceptable way out of what he is doing, and the teacher gets a way to carry on.

What Does a Classroom Based on Choice Look Like?

It's a team effort! Everyone is included. The beginning of the year involves establishing rules, routines, and rituals with the children. These are modeled and practiced. Then you must spend time building responsible children by asking more questions and giving fewer answers. When children pose questions, you turn them around with responses like these:

- What do you think?
- What are your choices?
- Which choice would be best?
- Which choice could you make and be okay with?

The question from a child could be as simple as "What should I do with my wet boots?" If it's established that wet boots belong on the tile in front of the child's cubby, you should not answer the question but instead ask, "What do you think you should do with them?" If a child says, "I don't have a pencil," you could respond, "What are your choices when you don't have a pencil?" A fellow educator once told me that if a child says, "I don't know," I should immediately reply, "Well, what would you say/do if you did know?" I am amazed at how often this will elicit a response. It usually turns out to be a perfectly appropriate answer to the very question the child posed.

Let's take a look at some other common classroom dilemmas. Let's say a child can't reach the shelf to put his lunch box on it and can't unzip his coat. He comes to you tugging on the coat and says, "The shelf is too high, and I can't unzip my coat." Many teachers simply take the lunchbox and place it up on the

Children begin to think of you as the answer to all of their challenges, even the small ones.

shelf, then bend down and begin to "take over the problem" of unzipping the coat.

But some teachers realize that these small actions may eventually cause a big problem. The big problem is that children begin to think of you as the answer to all of their challenges, even the small ones. Each small thing you do for them cements that notion in their minds, and eventually they start looking to you to solve every challenge they run into. They act completely helpless and unwilling to try—exactly the pattern of behavior that we come to loathe in children. And we've created this pattern if we've led children to believe that we're responsible for solving their problems.

Now, they're young, and I believe that we should treat them that way. We don't need to do everything for them, but we do need to support them in building a sense of responsibility. Let's examine how this might be a learning opportunity. When the child comes to you with the lunch box and zipper problem, you might ask, "What do you do if you can't reach the shelf?" If necessary, remind the child that he can use the step stool. Help him to find it and then use it to place his lunch box on the shelf.

Next, address the zipper on the coat. Remember, the child didn't ask you to fix it for him. He said, "I can't unzip my coat." At this point, I think you need to ask the child to state his options. Say, "What are your choices when you can't unzip your coat?" It's so enlightening to listen to a child come up with options. He might say, "I could pull it over my head, I could ask

When you allow children to make their own choices, you empower them.

you or a friend for help, or I could leave it on." If he can't come up with options on his own, guide him through the process.

You then can say, "Okay, you know your options. What are you going to do?" I can't tell you how many times children have sat in the classroom for extended periods of time with their coats on. Some people might question letting a child do that. But when you allow children to make their own choices, you empower them. They start to understand the concepts of choice and consequence, and they begin to feel capable of making choices. These are small life lessons that can make a big difference.

Just the Facts, Please

A good discipline plan includes a no-excuses policy and a state-the-facts approach. In addressing choices with children, use a matter-of-fact voice to point out that we all have excuses, but many of those excuses are the results of the choices we make. Therefore, if someone makes a bad choice, we don't need to know the excuse. In fact, the time spent on the excuse (which deals with the past and with things we can't change) detracts from finding a solution—making better choices now and in the future.

If a child hasn't completed his work and you feel you've given him ample time, accept *no excuses* for why it isn't done.

Then take time to *state the facts.* Establish what you know, what you need, and what the child needs to do, then ask when she feels that she can do it. Use a matter-of-fact voice to convey that you're not angry but are looking for a solution to the problem.

The conversation between the teacher and the student might sound like this:

Teacher: I see that you haven't finished the work that was assigned this morning. I feel that you didn't make a good choice in how you spent your time.

Student: Joe was talking to me. That's why I couldn't get it done. I was going to, but then I—

Teacher: I don't need to know why it isn't finished. I feel that you had time to do it. You didn't get it done for whatever the reason, and now I need you to finish it. What can you and I do to make that happen?

In some cases, you may need to ask the student specifically what her choices are when someone is talking to her and she's trying to work.

Positive Discipline Guidelines

You need to decide on the guidelines that are most important to you. Here are a few of mine.

Children & Adults Deserve to Be Heard

Communication involves interchange between people who send messages and people who receive them. If communication means that one person always does the talking and the other person always does the listening, someone is not getting a turn to be heard. Children need to understand that there is no relationship between raising your voice in a scream and being listened to and understood. Teachers must model the concept that we don't scream to get others' attention. In fact, sometimes the best thing we can do to gain full attention and be heard is to remain silent until the listener appears to be listening. As mentioned earlier, it takes two people to argue. Be sure that as the adult, you don't let a conversation with a child turn into a power struggle.

Flexibility Is Key

Sometimes things need to be written in stone, and sometimes we can use a whiteboard so that we can modify or delete things. For example, think about a situation in which you planned to do something at a specific time but the plan didn't quite work out. As adults we can become frustrated by this kind of change, and children are no different. But flexibility is important to scheduling and planning, and it's also a life skill. Teach children to accept that "life happens," so we need to deal with change and make the most of it. If gym is canceled because the gym teacher is ill, we may be sad, but we need to try to understand that this is a circumstance beyond our control. Being angry or sad won't help. Instead, encourage children to brainstorm what the class could do with the time they were supposed to be in gym.

Life & Classrooms Are Filled with Opportunities to Negotiate

It's also imperative to show children that there are times when people negotiate—times when we must weigh the most

Children need to know that they don't have to give in to be part of the team.

important thing against things that are less important to us. Negotiating with others is a life skill that allows us to gain something without losing everything. If you want the same box of crayons as another student, the two of you might decide to share or take turns. If you want *all* the colors, you may need to take turns with the box. If you're willing to use one color while the other student uses a different color, you may want to share. You can't both decide that you'll take the box and keep it for yourself.

Opportunities for debate and voting are ever present in classrooms as people assert their right to choose, but it's important to teach children that the outcome might not always be their first choice. I am saddened by the number of children who have an all-or-nothing attitude. These are the children whose point of view is, "If we don't do it the way I want, I won't do it at all." Negotiating can be a fine art and one that will serve children well in life. Let's teach them to be willing to work things out together.

Some Things Can Be Negotiated. Some Things Can't.

Children also need to know that they don't have to give in to be part of the team. If a friend tells you to run your skateboard over a neighbor's new lawn and you say no, he might try to negotiate with you. He might say, "Okay, just ride your bike

Teachers tell me that there are days when they can't stand to hear their names called one more time.

across it instead." You don't have to negotiate with the friend. You can say, "I'm not willing to do that." It's good to be flexible and to be a person who's willing to bend. But there are also times when it's okay to say, "This is not negotiable."

Problem Solving Is a Learned Skill

Children need a supportive atmosphere if they're going to learn to solve problems. They can be taught to think things through so that they can make appropriate choices and come up with solutions to problems. As teachers, we can present children with small problems to solve each day so that they have the right skills when the big problems come along.

Think of the small things we do for children and turn them into opportunities to help them problem solve. If a child comes to you and says, "I can't fold my paper," you should reply, "What are you going to do?" Don't be so quick to fold it for him. If he says, "I don't know," ask him, "What are your choices?" He might reply that one choice is to ask you. In that case, I would say to the child, "Yes, you could ask me using a question and your manners. What else could you do?" I am constantly surprised when a child says, "I could try it myself," "I could ask a friend," or "I could sit here with my paper not folded." Ask him, "What would you like to do?" I can't tell you how many times the child has asked a friend instead of me. The problem was solved, and I didn't solve it for him.

Teachers tell me that there are days when they can't stand to hear their names called one more time. This business of turning to the teacher for everything isn't good for you, and it isn't good for the children either. If you're always solving their problems, you're building dependency, not teaching problem solving. When you constantly jump in and rescue your students, it teaches them to look to you—rather than to themselves—for solutions.

Many, many times I see teachers address the small problems that come up by doing *for* the child whatever it is that needs doing. The teacher ties the shoe, gets another pencil, folds the paper, or unzips the coat. When I ask teachers why they do this, they often reply, "It's quicker and easier to just do it." Well, maybe in this one instance it is, but what about over the long term? Add up the minutes spent "just doing it," and I bet you'll find that it would have taken much less time to teach children the skill or ask them to problem solve.

Teachers spend too much time on short-term fixes to long-term problems. You know the saying about giving someone a fish versus teaching him to fish? The second alternative will give the person a strategy that she can use her entire life. Start the year with a rubber ball in your pocket and ask yourself how you can bounce each problem or question back to the students. Here are some possibilities.

Child: May I get another piece of paper?
Teacher: What's our rule about getting paper when you need it?

Child: I don't have a pencil.
Teacher: What do you do if you don't have a pencil?

Child: I can't find my journal.

Teacher: I like to put things in specific places. Do you do that? I don't know where your journal is, but what will you need to do to find it?

Child: Carter said that Taylor said that Mark doesn't like me.

Teacher: Carter, Taylor, Mark, and you! I didn't hear my name in there, so I must not be involved. What are you going to do?

Teaching Social Skills Is a Vital Part of Education

Creating a plan for the social and emotional atmosphere of a classroom is as important as, if not more important than, creating good plans for reading, writing, math, and other subjects. Children who lack social skills lack the ability to work in a group atmosphere, and sometimes social skills must be learned. You can't assume that children have or should have them prior to coming into your class.

Be a Coach, Not a Police Officer

Think of the responsibilities of a police officer: enforcing laws, imposing penalties, controlling crowds, stopping traffic. Now think of the responsibilities of a coach: helping children to learn rules, teaching them to use the correct strategies, assisting them when needed, supporting them in carrying through. Which is our role as educators?

Building problem-solving skills calls on the ability to guide, assist, and support children in finding a good path. That's a much different role than that of a police officer. Let's be coaches, not police officers.

When you offer your students choices, often you give them a sense of freedom.

Structured Choice & the Brain

Offering choices builds motivation to learn, and that includes learning self-control. By offering choices, you're telling children, "You are capable of choosing. You are a responsible person." Choices are also good for the brain. When you believe that you're making a choice and that you have some control over a decision, your stress level goes down. You've probably experienced that in your own life, and the same thing applies to the children you teach. When you offer your students choices, often you give them a sense of freedom. Most people thrive on that. The brain doesn't do well with ultimatums; it prefers options, not demands.

Now I'm not advocating allowing children to make every choice in the classroom. But I do believe in the importance of offering choices in general. The alternatives should always be ones that you, as the responsible adult, can live with. For example, you might ask students, "Who wants to do word building on a sheet of paper, and who wants to play Boggle?" That's a structured choice. It's basically the *same* choice, but children will hear the choice and engage their brains to decide what they want to do. Of course, often children will choose the option that they perceive to be more fun. Isn't that great, if the children are motivated to carry out the activity?

Consequence vs. Punishment

I offer the following scenario. My husband was called to work early one morning when I was out of town. He contacted my niece to go to our home and wake up our two teenagers for school. She called me a bit after arriving to say that my daughter had gotten out of bed and was in the shower getting ready for school. My son, however, had made a different choice. As soon as he saw his cousin, the first words out of his mouth were, "Where's Dad?" She said, "He was called to work early." My son quickly replied, "Cool. I'm not going to school. I need a mental health day."

My niece was concerned that my husband would be upset about my son not going to school. I asked her if she could physically pick up my 250-pound, 6-foot 5-inch son and carry him to school. (She is 5 feet 4 inches with heels.) She replied, "No!" I then told her to go back upstairs and to say to my son, who was still in bed, "Your mom and dad want you to go to school, but ultimately it's your choice." She did. He said, "Good," and rolled over. He didn't go to school that day.

I arrived home several days later. I asked my son if he'd been sick on the morning his cousin had called me. He said, "No." I replied, "So you just decided that you wanted a day off?" He said, "Yes," and tried to continue on with how tired he was. He told me that he'd had two classes that weren't very important that day and had an extra study hall, so he didn't miss much.

I reminded him that I didn't need to know all of that. It was a simple question: had he decided to take the day off? He replied, "Yes." I asked, "Would you have made that choice if your father and/or I had been here?" He said, "No." I told him I needed his car keys for the rest of the week.

Aren't many of our punishments self-inflicted, the consequences of the choices we make?

Now my son has lived with my "natural consequence" statements (I like to say that I avoid punishments) long enough that he challenges my thoughts, and he wanted to know the justification for my decision. I told him, "This is in no way a punishment; it is a natural consequence of the choice you made. The way I see it, you acted irresponsibly. Therefore, I'm afraid to allow you to drive a large vehicle to school. What if you choose to act irresponsibly again? What might happen to you, the car, or someone else?" I went on to explain that I just couldn't live with myself if that happened and wouldn't want to inflict that guilt on him either. Irresponsible sixteen-year-olds need their moms to protect them. He shook his head and said, "I'm now convinced that you can make any punishment seem like a natural consequence!"

In reality, aren't many of our punishments self-inflicted, the consequences of the choices we make? Suppose you lie to a friend. The next time the friend asks you something and seems leery of your answer, that friend is not punishing you for lying but is in fact responding to your previous choice to be deceitful.

Natural Consequences

It's essential for children to learn that their actions and words lead to natural consequences. Consequences are part of life. At times, a child may make choices that result in punishments; you need to determine when that's appropriate.

I can't change the fact that the child hits, but I can ensure that he doesn't have the *opportunity* to hit.

Often the natural consequence may be punishment enough. For example, it's important to point out to children who hit others that this is an unacceptable behavior and that since others don't like to be hit, the child doing the hitting will need to be removed from the group. I can't change the fact that the child hits, but I can ensure that he doesn't have the *opportunity* to hit. Empower the child by stating, "This is a consequence of the choice you made."

Another example of a consequence could be when a child loses free time because she doesn't use her work time wisely. Some people view this as a punishment. If it is, it's self-inflicted. Each of us decides how to use our time. If we don't use it wisely, we must reallocate time to take care of the original task that wasn't finished. I'm sure that at times this seems like a punishment, but in truth it's a consequence. What if I say I'll mow the lawn on Saturday but decide to put it off and do it the next day? If I then get invited to a picnic and can't go because I have to mow the lawn—work I didn't do when I had the time—who inflicted the punishment? Can this actually be viewed as a consequence of the choice I made?

Children need to be aware that many things that "happen to us" are actually the results of our choices. Don't ever let them put the responsibility on you. A child who's told to use free time to complete work that should have been finished earlier might say, "You're mean. You took my playtime." You must then say,

"Oh, no, I didn't make that choice. Losing free time was a result of the choice you made."

Think of the child who throws Jell-O in the cafeteria at lunchtime. What is the natural consequence? If you throw Jell-O, you clean up the mess. The consequence truly is a result of the child's actions and choices. This takes the responsibility off the teacher and puts it on the child. Taking responsibility for our own actions is a very important lesson!

Is Punishment Warranted?

If there doesn't seem to be a natural consequence, you may feel that a punishment is warranted. In this case, keep in mind the following questions.

- Does the punishment make sense?
  Is it appropriate for the specific infraction? Be careful about using one-size-fits-all punishments.

- Does the child understand what's happening?
  Has there been an explanation of why this punishment is being imposed? Has there been a discussion of what will happen next time?

- Does it reduce the undesirable behavior and increase the desirable behavior?
  If it doesn't, should you consider a different approach?

- Does it lead to learning?
  If the punishment doesn't lead to learning, is it effective?

If anyone thinks that someone needs to lose, you're dealing with a no-win situation.

- Does it leave both the teacher's and the child's self-respect intact?

  No one likes to "lose face." It's important that both the teacher and the child be treated with respect. If anyone thinks that someone needs to lose, you're dealing with a no-win situation.

- Is it really a punishment, or is it an empty threat?

  My mom often would lose her temper with the four girls in our family when we bickered and physically fought with one another. (How she stayed sane, I will never know.) She used to say, "I'm going to pay someone to take you" or "I'm going to ground you for the rest of your life." Now, I'm not positive, but I'd be willing to bet that no one would have taken us (even for money). And even at the time I was pretty sure that she wouldn't be able to ground me for the rest of my life, as I didn't plan on staying in her house for that long. She saw these statements as threats of punishment. We knew she couldn't follow through on those threats, so they were just words.

I believe that the ultimate question you must ask yourself before inflicting any punishment on a child is, "How would I feel if this were done to me?" Asking that question might avoid a lot of the animosity and thoughts of vengeance we sometimes stir up in children.

Teaching About Consequences

Here are a few other topics to consider when you're teaching about consequences.

Making Amends

Children must learn that there are times when we need to make amends for the choices we make. If you intentionally break something, you should replace it. If you intentionally hurt someone's feelings and you feel bad about it, you can make amends by apologizing.

Encouraging Appropriate Behavior

Instead of telling children you'll punish a particular behavior, it's much better to explain to them that you realize they're having a hard time with that behavior. For example, if children are running in the hall, explain that walking in the hall is a safety issue. Let them know that this is a school rule that you thought they understood. Explain that perhaps it would help to practice this behavior. You can find many opportunities to inform children that they may need to practice certain appropriate behaviors. For instance, using mean language may indicate that a child doesn't know how to express emotions and use appropriate language; maybe she needs to practice these skills.

Mapping Choices

When a child behaves inappropriately, it's helpful to ask, "What could you have done?" Often, though, the child will respond, "I don't know." I believe that sometimes children really *don't* know. Mapping choices with a child allows her to explore

DISCOVERING OPTIONS

As you guide a child in discovering alternatives to a bad choice, the conversation might include some of these points.

Option taken:

• Cheated because I wasn't sure of the answer

Other options:

• Cry

• Study so that I might have felt confident

• Talk to the teacher

• Refuse to take the test

options beyond the one she chose. It's hard for young children to grasp that there are other alternatives. Developing a list of choices for specific examples illustrates how important it is to examine all of your choices before making one—in other words, to think things through. You might point out that if someone chooses to cheat on a test, that's not a good choice. Ask, "What might some other choices be?" Allow the child to identify any and all the choices that come to mind. Facilitate a conversation with her that puts other options on the table.

Once the child has identified options, you can review the options together and decide which ones would actually have helped the situation. Crying wouldn't have helped. Refusing to take the test would probably have led to more problems. Guide the child to the options that would have been more appropriate. Ask, "If you had studied, would you have felt better prepared, less unsure? More willing to trust what you knew?" Also, "Even if it still had been difficult, would it have helped to talk to the teacher? Possibly, you could have had additional time to prepare." Always ask the child what he feels would have been appropriate options.

The Verbal Reprimand

Sometimes people are verbally reprimanded for the choices they make. A bad choice is identified, and the person is told that it's not appropriate. If a child kicks stones on the playground

but doesn't hit anything or anyone, you might point out the behavior and ask the child to stop. This can be an effective way to identify a bad choice, and you can then guide the child in figuring out what she needs to do next.

Loss or Postponement of a Privilege

Sometimes our behaviors result in the loss or postponement of a privilege. If a child doesn't behave in class, it may be necessary to exclude that child from an assembly in the auditorium. Be sure to present this as a direct result of the choice the child made. You might explain that if the child can't behave in class, you can't possibly take her to the assembly with so many other children. Another example might be a time when work needs to be finished because the child chose not to complete it earlier in the day. This can result in postponing recess for the child. I'm not a fan of totally eliminating recess or free time; every child needs fresh air, space, and exercise. But it's acceptable to postpone recess for the child.

Keep in mind that loss or postponement of a privilege is an opportunity to point out how the child's choice impacted the future. In visiting a detention hall, I once asked a group of students why they weren't able to go on a field trip. I was intrigued by the responses. One student said, "I'm here and not on the field trip because of the school's dumb referral system." Another student said, "I was left at school for running away twice prior to the trip." The first student put the blame on the "outside." He

felt that he was being punished by the system that controlled him. He never identified what he had done, only what had been done to him. The second student took responsibility for the results of her actions. She understood that making the choice to run away had led the teacher to believe that she couldn't be trusted not to run away on the trip and that this was a chance the teacher couldn't take.

When the results of our behavior are negative, isn't it easier to blame something or someone on the outside instead of looking within ourselves? I desperately wanted the first child to identify his role in losing the privilege. It was important for him to understand that his actions had a result and that he was the one responsible for that result. The responsibility didn't belong to the person who wrote the referrals. This is another life lesson that children need assistance with: learning to take responsibility often means admitting that what is happening now was in our control to begin with. That's a tough lesson.

Building & Understanding Choice

When a child is born, the parents want to take care of her and to ensure that her every need is met. She's completely dependent on them. Once the child gains some independence and heads off to school, it's time to develop her understanding of freedom of choice and to instill in her a sense of what that freedom entails.

Good Choice vs. Bad Choice Scenarios

Adults have many opportunities to help children to see that their decisions often have good or bad outcomes. It's best to think out our choices and make the best one we can in each situation. Children need to see and hear what the outcomes might have been if they had made other choices. Many times, a child will make a bad choice and will tell you that she didn't know what would happen; she didn't understand the consequence. That's why it's necessary to voice, and possibly show, what might happen in a particular situation if the best choice isn't made.

Let's say that a child must wait his turn for the slide. Most of the time, the rule on playgrounds across America is that you

wait at the bottom of the ladder until the person gets to the top and begins the motion of sliding down. But why do we say this is the rule? Stating the rule isn't always enough, as some children might wonder what would happen if they didn't wait. (Or they won't wonder at all and just won't wait!) We need to explore why it is important to wait. Explain—or get the children to figure out—some of the reasons for choosing to wait at the bottom of the ladder. One reason might be that you might get kicked by the person in front of you if you follow too closely. Another reason might be that you don't want to be in the way in case the person slips. If you make the bad choice not to follow the rule, it might lead to you or someone else getting hurt.

Showing children the possible repercussions of their choices can help them to think things through before deciding what to do. As adults, most of us have learned to make decisions based on past experiences. Children don't always have the experience to decide which is the best choice. Before a child makes a bad choice, adults can assist him in thinking out the options. This can support children in recognizing that just about every situation involves choices—some of them appropriate and some not.

What Are My Choices?

Listing positive choices for a variety of situations empowers children to see that there are multiple choices—some good, some bad. Each person must decide which is most appropriate at a given time, in a given situation. What are my choices if I don't like what's being served for dinner? What are my choices when I arrive at school in the morning?

Some children will tell you that they have *no* choice. I like to remind them that we all have choices, but that many times we have learned which choices not to make. That makes it seem as if we have no choice because we know what we must do. This is a good thing! We know that if we find money on the street, we have several choices. We could keep it and tell people, we could keep it and hide it, or we could try to return it. I love to hear a child say, "You don't have a choice. You need to give it back." That shows discipline; the child knows her choices but she doesn't need to think them out because she knows which choice

If we choose to be dishonest, a possible effect might be that people don't trust us.

is the right thing to do. Never confuse having the right to make a choice with the idea that it's okay to make choices that are not right.

Cause & Effect

Learning that our actions and words lead to outcomes is what choice is all about. Many states' standards require that children in grades K–3 be able to identify cause and effect. Life teaches us this rule every day. Are we willing to live with the effects of a choice we make? If we choose to be dishonest, a possible effect might be that people don't trust us. Many of our choices determine how people treat us and what others think of us. The choices we make have short-term and long-term consequences. Ask children to think of a choice they might need to make about school. Work with them to create a list of possible actions, then ask the children to describe what the effects of each action could be. This will allow children to think beyond the immediate choice to the possible effects of the choice, now or later.

An easy illustration of this point might be to ask children what choices they have in this scenario.

Your teacher tells you that you may borrow one book from the classroom library each night. To do that, you need to put the title, your name, and the date on a certain form attached to a clipboard.

You want children to understand that each effect is caused by the choice they make.

What might your choices be?

- Don't borrow any books.
- Borrow a book and don't fill out the form.
- Borrow two or more books.
- Borrow a book, fill out the form, and cross off your name when you bring the book back.
- Borrow a book, fill out the form, and don't cross off your name when you bring the book back.
- Borrow a book and never return it.

Now look at the possible effect(s) of each choice. You want children to understand that each effect is caused by the choice they make.

- Don't borrow any books.
  - You don't have to worry about bringing them back.
  - You don't have a chance to reread any of the books at home that you read at school.

- Borrow a book and don't fill out the form.
  - You take the book home and bring it back.
  - You take the book home and don't bring it back. No one will know because you didn't list it.
  - You get caught and aren't able to borrow any more books.

- Borrow two or more books.
  — You get to take the books home and enjoy them.
  — You get caught taking more than one and lose the privilege of borrowing classroom books.

- Borrow a book, fill out the form, and cross off your name when you bring the book back.
  — You follow the rules.
  — You make the teacher happy.
  — You and the teacher feel good about your following the rules and know that this is acting responsibly.
  — You're secure knowing that following the rules allows you to continue to borrow classroom books.

- Borrow a book, fill out the form, and don't cross off your name when you bring the book back.
  — The teacher will be looking for you.
  — Other children might say you had the book last.
  — There might be a question about when and if you actually returned the book.

- Borrow a book and never return it.
  — You don't get to take any other books home.
  — You're not able to borrow any materials.
  — You're considered irresponsible.
  — The teacher is sad.
  — You admit that you lost the book and offer to pay for it.

So many choices, so many options. Children need to know that the choices they make often result in real outcomes.

In the end, unless you were threatened or incapacitated, you need to admit that you made that choice.

Responsibility

Taking responsibility means holding yourself answerable or accountable—recognizing that what happens is something that, to a large extent, you can control. We often want to blame someone or something else when we make a bad choice, but we must learn to take responsibility. In the end, unless you were threatened or incapacitated, you need to admit that you made that choice. Sometimes outside factors may lead to or even justify a bad choice, but it's imperative to remember that it was still a choice.

CORNERSTONE #3: COMMUNICATION

As adults we often tend to "talk at" children. Sure, there are times when it's necessary for us to tell them exactly what it is that we want or need, but if you want commitment on both sides, remember that your communication also needs to be two-sided. How many times have you thought, "Oh, that child wasn't listening"? If you're doing all the talking and I'm a child who has no role in the communication, then I must choose whether to listen or not. At this point, many children just tune out. You might as well be Charlie Brown's teacher: "Wa wa wa wa."

If we want children to take an active role in their learning, we must give them the opportunity to get involved in the process. We need to engage them in communication and encourage them to become active participants. We need to talk *with* them. That means keeping our statements short and our questions open so that we don't lose them in the communication.

For example, suppose a child is teasing another child. You might ask, "What are you doing?" or "How is what you're doing helping you or Miguel?" If the child responds with "Nothing" or "It's not," the situation might be quickly resolved. Any other answer would warrant a statement from you. If the child says, "I'm talking to my friend Miguel," you could say, "Are you using kind language?" and "Does Miguel want to continue to talk to you?" If the child says, "I don't know," you could reply, "If you don't know, how can you find out?" Ask questions such as "What should you do now?" and "When will you do that?"

Statements that go on too long seem like lectures to children. That kind of "talking at" children doesn't help them learn to think and communicate their thinking. To involve them and allow them the opportunity to learn, you must interact with them.

Communication Skills for Young Children

Children don't come to school with great social and communication skills for dealing with their peers. Often their skills are based on their past dealings with adults, siblings, or friends. Now they're in a room in which they're expected to interact with many more individuals in a setting that may have only one adult. As a child, I need to learn to speak to other children, to communicate what I think and feel. Children who have been

Children need to know how to say what they mean and mean what they say; that's a life skill.

"talked at" will expect you to do the talking. When you ask a question, these children often will respond with "I don't know." Their brains have not been wired to think—just to listen and take in. Now we're asking for communication, and they're at a loss. What's wrong with this picture?

Communication skills can and should be taught in classrooms. Children need to know how to say what they mean and mean what they say; that's a life skill. One way to start is with a lesson in expressing your thoughts, focusing on something as simple as saying "No" or "I don't like that!"

Some children are at a loss when it comes to dealing with other children who are saying or doing things they don't like. Their silence allows others to take advantage of them. Empower children with words so that they can express what they need and/or want. I tell children that when another child says, "I'm going to take that book now," it's okay to say, "No, I'm still using it." When someone says, "I want you to push the merry-go-round," I teach them that it's okay to say, "I don't want to push the merry-go-round."

You need to teach specific language for these situations. Attacking a person is never a good start to a healthy conversation. One of the first things I tell children is to learn to say things such as "I heard . . . ," "I felt . . . ," "I need . . . ," "I didn't like . . . ," or "I want . . . ," as opposed to making a statement that invites confrontation. If someone takes your spot on the car-

pet when you are in the bathroom, you can choose to handle this in one of two ways:

First, you can say, "You carpet hog! You are in my spot!" This is not the most effective way to get what you want (your spot back).

Second, you can say, "I needed to use the bathroom, and now you're in my spot. Can you please move so that I can sit back down?" This might not work—the other child could say no—but you will have done your best not to escalate a confrontation.

Will people always do what you want? Absolutely not! But I guarantee that your rate of success will be higher if you use your negotiation skills.

Talk. Don't Argue.

You also need to pay attention to how you're communicating with your students. It's important to remember not to argue with them. What you probably will need to do is talk with them, which is a very different thing. When you talk with a child who's upset—making sure the conversation is two-sided—you can often help the child to identify the emotion he's feeling and to recognize that this is a discussion that can take place when the emotion is under control. It's easy to understand why it wouldn't be a good idea to try to talk with a child who's extremely angry; that can quickly escalate to a power struggle. But it's just as important to realize that communication can be difficult when a child feels intimidated, scared, or nervous. Those are all very real emotions that will override the brain's ability to think things out.

Vocabulary That Works

The younger the child, the more important it is to use vocabulary that she knows and understands. As adults we like to say things such as "That's rude." But think about it: saying something like that to a young child may not give the child much information. It assumes that she knows the meaning of the word *rude*, and that's not necessarily the case. I once asked a child what *rude* meant. He answered, "You know, 'You rude your bike yesterday.'" I think it's a safe bet that this child had no idea what I meant when I said it was rude for him to tell the child next to him that she smelled.

Telling a child to be kind seems like a positive request that the child should understand. But to be kind, you must understand what kindness is and what it isn't. Just saying "Be kind" implies that the child knows what being kind entails. In many instances, he may not. What if the child is being raised in a home where there are few kind acts, if any? What if the child hasn't seen manners modeled or learned how to ask for something in a polite way? What if he isn't spoken to in a kind tone at home? How can he be expected to be kind? Too often we assume knowledge. Instead, we must find out what children know. Then we must teach them the things that they don't know and that we expect and value.

Proximity to a child conveys the message that the child is important.

Positive Language = Positive Results

Many times teachers use directives that emphasize what we *don't* want. Focusing instead on what we *do* want enables us to turn our statements into more positive language that can work wonders with children.

Which would you rather hear?

This?	Or This?
Don't run in the halls.	Please use walking feet in the halls.
No yelling out.	We need to raise our hands to speak so that we can take turns and be heard.
Get off the yellow line.	Please stand behind the yellow line for your safety and the safety of those around you.
Don't be mean.	Please be kind.
Don't waste materials.	Use our materials wisely.
No hitting.	Keep your hands and feet to yourself.
Quit goofing around.	I need you to pay attention.

In changing these statements, we focus on the positives of what we want or need as opposed to the negatives. This builds communication skills and teaches children to make statements that are less confrontational. It changes the whole tone of the communication. The message is the same, but using a more positive approach increases your chances of getting compliance.

The Power of Proximity

Calling across the room is not acceptable behavior for children or teachers. Important messages are personal, and that means you can best deliver them by getting close to the child you're communicating with. Proximity to a child conveys the message that the child is important. If you're close to the child, you can "get down on her level," making eye contact and putting yourself in a less authoritative position. This also gives you the possibility of touching a child's shoulder or hand when you talk. Many times, just touching a child will get her attention and make the communication more personal.

Knowing When NOT to Communicate

I believe that knowing when not to communicate is as important as knowing how to communicate. Sometimes situations and feelings escalate, and a child and/or an adult needs time without any communication—time to think out the situation and to make plans for dealing with it. The "time-out" is one of the most positive options we have, and it can take on any name that allows it to be seen in a positive light. Remember, high emotion = low problem solving. It's important to recognize when we need time to think, to identify emotions, or just to cool down.

Time-out is a tried-and-true strategy for both parents and teachers. It's a method that acknowledges the importance of think time. Unfortunately, it's become more of a punishment than a solution. I have actually witnessed parents dragging children to a time-out spot and sitting on the children to keep them there. I'm not sure, but I imagine that it would be hard for a child to think of solutions to a problem with someone sitting on her.

If you want to employ time-out, you need to address it in a more positive way, making sure children understand what you're trying to accomplish and what their role will be. Find a quiet, out-of-the-way place and designate that space as a time-out area.

TIME TO RENAME THE TIME-OUT AREA

Every classroom needs a time-out area. But you don't have to call it that! You could refer to it as:

- The Think Tank
- I Need a Minute (Or Two)
- The Quiet Zone
- Seconds for Solutions
- Meeting with Myself
- Reasoning Region
- The Stress-Free Spot
- The Chamber of Choice
- Downtime
- Reflection
- I Could . . .
- Focus Time
- Pondering Place

In the long term, children are able to solve problems better when they're given time to think.

It's a sure sign that a child needs a time-out when he is:

- Continuously moody
- Extremely frustrated
- Angry
- Irrational
- Overly emotional (sobbing, screaming, out-of-control goofy)
- Unwilling to communicate in an attempt to identify either the problem or a solution

These are real expressions of real feelings children have. Adults need to recognize when any of these signs are present and the chances of engaging in valuable communication with a child are low or nonexistent. We all want a quick fix, but knowing when to wait is a gift. In the long term, children are able to solve problems better when they're given time to think and to deal with their emotions. We will revisit time-out in our toolbox of management techniques.

When Is It Their Turn to Talk?

When teachers complain about disruptive classroom behaviors, I often see "children talking (communicating) out of turn" and "children constantly talking (communicating)" at the top of the list. And yet if children don't learn to express themselves

I'll figure out very quickly that the only way I'll be heard is if I yell out or talk out of turn.

and learn to talk to one another, we as a society lose. Here's food for thought. Children come to school, and we spend a great deal of time shushing them. There are too many of them to let them all talk. Yet if we are going to tell children that *we* need time to talk, we must allow *them* time to talk. So when teachers tell me they have a problem with children talking at inappropriate times, my first question is, "When in the day is it their turn to talk?"

Let's look at this from a child's perspective. I come to school, and they tell me to be quiet. The teacher says I must raise my hand to speak and that talking out of turn is disruptive. But realistically, I know I'm competing with twenty-plus kids when I raise my hand. What are the chances that I'll actually be chosen? Don't you think I'll figure out very quickly that the only way I'll be heard is if I yell out or talk out of turn?

Do we not realize that when we ask too much and don't give enough, we force children to do what we so desperately want them *not* to? These are *children*.

If I asked you to honestly assess how often you ask a question of the class and then call on one of the first three students who raise their hands, what would your answer be? Would it be 10 percent, 30 percent, 50 percent, or more of the time? As teachers we even disguise how often we choose one of the first three students. We say things such as "Ashley, I know you know the answer, but let's give everyone time." Two seconds later, we say, "Okay, Ashley, go ahead. We have to get going." We teach children to get a hand in the air as quickly as possible, or they will have no chance of getting to respond.

Processing the question and formulating an answer takes time. We tend to say we have no time, but think of how much time has been wasted when children don't think but instead just get their hands up. Have you ever had this happen? You ask a question, hands go up (sometimes before the children even know the question), you call on a child, and she sits there with a blank stare, mumbling, "Uhhh . . . Uhhh . . ." You ask, "Do you know the answer?" and the child responds, "I forgot." We've taught children to rush to be included instead of taking time to think about the question. Each of us is a social being who wants to be heard. How do we find a way to make sure the children in our classrooms are heard? We begin by being proactive.

Being proactive means that you explain to children that if everyone talks, no one is heard; that in a large group, they must take turns. You add that when a question is asked, they will have "think time." This will not require hands in the air, because hands in the air don't help our brains to engage. You explain

that sometimes you will put them in small groups so that they will have more of an opportunity to contribute and talk. And you emphasize that in this classroom, it's important to share. Therefore, each hour you will give the children one or two minutes when they can talk to one another.

Many children who struggle with calling out can be taught that they'll have an opportunity to talk and that they must have self-control. But you need to ensure that they're heard, that there's time for them to talk. If you don't give children a chance to talk, they will talk anyway—just not always when you want them to. Let's make sure that our children not only learn good communication skills for a variety of situations but also have a chance to practice them.

Nonverbal Signals

Nonverbal signals can give you a way to communicate with the whole class and with individual children. Perhaps you wear a tie when you want the children to stay away from your desk or table. Tell them that you're "all tied up" and that unless it's an emergency, questions or visiting must wait.

There are all sorts of variations on this theme. I once observed a teacher wearing a Hawaiian lei. The children informed me that she was "on vacation" and they could contact her only with a postcard. If they had a question that wasn't an emergency, they could write it down and put it on her desk. This method seemed to eliminate a lot of unnecessary questions, and I'm certain that the children who did write down their questions were gaining skills in communicating via pencil and paper.

In my own classroom, I once told the children that we needed a signal only our class understood. The signal we developed was tapping your head twice and touching your nose when things were going well and/or you saw someone doing a good job. Whenever I used the signal, the children would laugh and smile, knowing that I thought they were doing a good job and also knowing that this was "our" unique signal.

Some teachers get students' attention with hand-clapping patterns that the children must repeat back, or they may blow a

whistle or turn out the lights for silence. It's also good to have picture clues that remind children of classroom rules or "time of day" (work time, playtime, visiting time, and so on). The pictures are a valuable alternative to using your voice, and they also last longer!

Hand signals work, too. I've visited schools where three fingers up means children should be quiet (closed mouths), with eyes forward and "listening ears on." An adult starts the signal, and as soon as someone else notices, she follows, lifting her hand with three fingers showing. Soon everyone in the entire room has three fingers up, voice "off," eyes front, and "listening ears on."

You can also use nonverbal signals with individual children. Maybe you give a thumbs-up to let a child know you've noticed that he's staying on task. If you develop a special signal, the children will respond with enthusiasm.

Label the Behavior, Not the Child

Do you see any difference between the following two statements?

1. "You are a liar!"
2. "When you don't tell the truth, it's called lying. That's what you're doing right now."

Here are two more:

1. "You are a big bully!"
2. "When you talk to a friend in that tone of voice, using those words, you are bullying her."

Think about some of the labels we hear used in school and at home. We label a child a "thief" if he steals, a "brat" if he's unruly or defiant, "bossy" if he's demanding or domineering, and "lazy" if he's averse to work. If a child uses a loud voice or talks over others, she's a "big mouth"; if she starts complaining, she's a "whiner"; if she daydreams, she's a "space cadet"; and if she tattles, she's a "tattletale." The problem is that these labels define behaviors. But behaviors do not define children, and labels can lead a child to believe that they do.

I remember a time when I asked a child, "Why did you lie?" He responded, "Because I'm a liar. My dad says so." A child will live up to a label. We must be careful to identify behaviors and the power the child has to change those behaviors without applying labels that are very hard to overcome. In this child's situation, it would be much more appropriate to say, "What you did was to not tell the truth, and that's called lying."

Identify Feelings

Emotions drive our behavior. When we're angry, we withdraw or lash out. When we're happy, we smile and show enthusiasm. With children, the connection is pretty easy to see:

emotions rule the way children behave. And yet it's often hard for young children to identify why they're doing what they're doing. This is directly related to the difficulty a child has in identifying emotions and in figuring out why a particular behavior is connected to those emotions.

Learning to identify and manage our emotions is a huge step toward controlling the behaviors that go with them. To build good communication skills, it's imperative that you help children translate what they feel into appropriate words. For example, children often express emotions by saying that they're "mad," "sad," or "happy." But often when a child says that he's mad, he's really reacting to feelings of frustration or hurt. If you help children to identify their true emotions and the steps they can take to deal with those emotions, you'll go a long way toward building positive behaviors.

Turn Negatives into Positives

Isn't there a fine line between negative and positive behaviors in the real world? Aren't some of the behaviors we think of as negative when we see them in children the same ones that we consider quite valuable in adults? Take a look at the box on page 98. I think the real concern shouldn't be eliminating all of these behaviors but instead refocusing some of the behaviors to make them more acceptable in the classroom—and in life.

I know something about this from my own experience. I can't tell you how many teachers have commented on the high level of energy I have in presentations. Some remark that they're jealous that I seem to run in high gear all the time. When I was a child, that energy level wasn't always seen as a positive! But one teacher

(continued on page 99)

A TRAIT BY ANY OTHER NAME

Sometimes, it's all in how you look at things. Here are a few examples.

The Child Is:	But Could Also Be Described As:	Who Is This?
Aggressive	Assertive	A person who can stand up for himself and others. He knows what he wants and needs and is willing to communicate those wants and needs.
Bossy	A leader	Someone with a take-charge attitude who gets things done. She is willing to step up to the plate in critical situations.
Defiant and strong willed	Determined	A mover and shaker! Someone who won't give up, no matter how long something takes or what obstacles he encounters.
Loud and talkative	Outgoing	A social butterfly who puts others at ease by starting and maintaining conversations. She's so friendly and is always the first to say hello. This may be the person who's willing to say things that others wish they could.
A wiggle worm	Energetic	A bundle of energy who is in constant motion, running circles around the rest of us.
An instigator	A devil's advocate	Someone who's not afraid to question and initiate debate. She keeps us all on our toes by reminding us to think.
Failing to follow directions	Thinking outside the box	Someone who's always willing to try something new and explore other possibilities.

High energy is something we discourage in children in classrooms but honor in adults.

(continued from page 97)

in particular recognized my inability to stay still for long periods. He would often send me on errands, sometimes even within the classroom, to help me learn to control some of that energy. Other times he would ask me to color, write, or play a game.

Today I'm frequently reminded of how he taught me to channel some of my energy. On long plane trips, I often bring books, games such as crossword or Sudoku, and my laptop for writing. Instead of constantly moving, I try to channel that urge by occupying my mind. It's funny that high energy is something we discourage in children in classrooms but honor in adults.

I'd suggest that we should be careful not to try to eliminate behaviors that are of value in life. Instead, let's focus on teaching children how best to exhibit these behaviors in positive ways. Many negative traits can be molded into positive traits by the right artist!

You Have the Right to Say That!

I've often felt that a friend of mine consistently makes poor choices in life. This includes everything from jobs, finances, and relationships to her habit of making excuses to herself. Keeping feelings locked up inside can lead to major upheavals later on. I

My friend decided she would work fewer days. Now this is fine if you can live on less money, but it's not okay if you can't pay your bills.

believe that at some point, it's necessary for all of us to be able to express how we feel.

I recall a time when my friend decided she wanted more time to herself, so she would work fewer days. Now this is fine if you can live on less money, but it's not okay if you can't pay your bills and you may soon need a new car. Several months later, my friend's car died, and she had no money and no plan. She asked for my assistance. I love her and was willing to help, but in this instance, I believed that poor choices had led to a problem of hers becoming a problem of mine. I needed to say, "I will help, but I resent that this is happening, as you could have made other choices that would have prevented me from having to be involved."

Let children know that we have the right to tell others how we feel. We may feel upset, put out, or aggravated, and we should be able to say so. Often hiding those feelings and not saying what we think can escalate a situation. Sometimes the next little thing that happens will set us off. Many people will say, "Well, what's her problem? It was such a small thing!" They don't realize that the reaction was really the result of several things.

Children should be allowed to voice their feelings and concerns in a positive manner. We often don't teach them the appropriate way to respond when they have negative feelings; we tend to focus on displaying only the positive emotions. But negative emotions exist, and children have the right to feel them and to express them. One of the most powerful tools adults have for conveying this concept is to model the appropriate behavior. When children are not following my directions, I might say, "I feel frustrated when you all choose to disregard what I've asked you to do." When a child is unkind to another classmate, I might say, "I feel disappointed that you would choose to treat another person the way you are right now."

Feelings run a gamut that could reach from the earth to the moon. There are so many feelings that come up in response to so many situations, and each of us must learn to express how we feel without worrying about whether the feeling is okay. Every feeling, good or bad, is okay. The best lesson is to learn to recognize our feelings and to communicate them in ways that are appropriate.

Building & Understanding Communication

When I entered college, my adviser asked me if I wanted to take a communications course. I remember thinking, "Are you kidding me? I have no problem communicating. Is there a course in being quiet?" Of course, I now realize that communication is so much more than just talking. Children's lessons in communication start when we smile and make silly faces at babies. Later, when they get to school, we constantly model many ways of communicating. But we can do better. Let's set a goal to enhance children's communication skills every day in our classrooms.

Identifying Responses That Accompany Emotions

Teach children to say, "I feel _____ when _____. I need/want _____."

You might give examples such as these:

- I feel sad when you call me names. I need you to stop doing that.
- I feel embarrassed when you try to trip me. I need you to keep your feet to yourself.
- I feel happy when you help me. I want you to know that I appreciate it.
- I feel excited when you include me. I want to say thanks.

Draw faces that express emotions and ask children what emotion each face might be expressing. Then ask why or when someone might feel that emotion. This type of activity allows children to explore specific emotions and what might cause each one. Then give students a chance to talk about how someone might handle that emotion. We may believe that we know how someone else feels, but we truly understand only how *we* feel. Communication often involves stating our beliefs and letting people know what "signal" we're receiving. Sometimes we're wrong; other times we're right on the money. But we all would communicate better if we learned to use language that expressed our beliefs and feelings.

Teach children to say, "You think it's _____. I think it's _____. _____." Come up with some examples together. They might include something like the following:

- You think it's funny. I think it's cruel. Please stop talking to me.
- You think it's right. I think it's wrong. I'm not going to do it.

Then I asked the children, "If I don't want to share them, is that unkind?" They all agreed that it was.

It's Not Just *What* You Say

Working with a classroom of children several years ago opened my eyes to a dilemma that exists in many schools. We often make blanket statements because they give us an easy way to explain things, but those statements sometimes confuse young children. For example, I was asking the children in this classroom to give me examples of kind versus unkind behavior in several situations. In one example, I told the children that they were on a swing and that all the other swings at the playground were broken. I said, "Now pretend that children are lining up next to the swing to get a turn. What might be a kind thing and an unkind thing to do in this situation?" The children did a great job of telling me to share the swing; some even offered to get a timer to keep the time equal for all the children. They volunteered that it would be *unkind* to stay on the swing and maybe even call out, "I'm never getting off!"

My next example was this: "I'm a child who has potato chips at snack time. You love my potato chips, and you ask if you can have some. What would be a kind thing or an unkind thing to do?" Right away, without any thought, the children chimed in and said, "Share them." Sharing is a basic concept that we value and hope to impart to our children. I had to think for a minute, but then I asked the children, "If I don't want to share them, is that unkind?" They all agreed that it was.

This kind of reaction worries me. I don't want children to believe that they have to share their snacks to be kind people.

I'm not saying that I condone hurtful behavior, but you can't make someone feel sorry.

You don't have to share your food to be kind. I pointed out to the children that how they answered the request was more important than whether or not they chose to share the chips. I told them that a person could say, "I brought this bag of chips for myself, and I want to eat them myself" or "My mom tells me not to share my snacks at school." There also may be a time when the kindest thing you can do, if you don't want to share or feel that you shouldn't share, is to eat the chips somewhere else or to put them away.

A scenario I *wouldn't* want to see would be one in which a child says that she doesn't want to share with one child and then turns around and gives a different child some of her chips. That, to me, would be unkind.

At times, when it comes to being kind, our words are as important as our actions. There may be many things that a child doesn't want to do. He can learn the language to express his feelings and still remain a kind person.

"Sorry!" Isn't Okay

Please, please, please . . . tell children there is no such word as "sorry!"— at least not by itself! This word is used and abused hundreds of times a day. A child calls another child a name, and I hear the teacher say, "That wasn't nice. Say you're sorry." The child says, "Sorry!" and runs away. It seems that this child isn't really sorry but just going through the motions of doing what the teacher asked, in order to get out of trouble.

If a person is truly sorry, then he should express it by addressing the other child personally and always using the words, "I'm sorry," not just "Sorry!" The word alone serves no purpose in mending the situation. The child should learn to look the other child in the eye and not only apologize but also tell her why he's apologizing. If the child is feeling sorrow for calling the other child a name, then a more appropriate statement would be, "I'm sorry I called you that name. It was unkind, and I feel bad that I hurt you."

This next statement is one that gets me in trouble all over the country: don't tell children that they *must* apologize. Now, I'm not saying that I condone name-calling and other hurtful behavior, but you can't make someone feel sorry. He may say the words, but that probably won't change his behavior or his beliefs.

Instead, I like to ask children what they think they should do when they do something that hurts another child. Sometimes they say they should apologize. I say, "If you think that's the right thing to do, then you should do it." However, if a child who's hurt another child doesn't come up with the idea himself or truly doesn't think he needs to apologize, I don't force him into it. I might mention that it could be helpful or a kind thing to do, but I don't insist on it.

If a child is unwilling to apologize or just doesn't feel that it's necessary, I try to put the power into the other child's hands. I turn my attention to that child and say something like, "I can see that you're hurt by the name Trent called you. I feel sad that

It bothers me to hear the child receiving the apology say, "It's okay."

he doesn't seem to care that you're hurt, but we can't make him a kinder person or change his actions. Only he can do that. You must decide how you'll react to him now. Maybe you'd prefer not to play with him." I think it's important to ask the child what her choices are if someone is unkind and is not sorrowful about it.

There's one thing that I think is worse. When a child is made to apologize, it bothers me to hear the child receiving the apology say, "It's okay." We've taught children to respond in this way. But is it okay if someone calls you a name or does something else to hurt you? No, it's not okay. I tell children not to say, "It's okay." They can say, "I accept your apology" or "I forgive you." Or they can acknowledge the apology without accepting it by saying "Thank you for apologizing." Children don't have to accept an apology, and it certainly is *not* okay.

Manners Matter

If you were raised in a household that valued good manners, it's difficult to understand people who seem to possess few, if any, manners. I once visited a classroom in which the children had met me a few hours prior to the visit. I knew that they'd been told my name but chances were that some of them might have forgotten it. I was at a table with a group of children, and one said, "Hey, you [pointing at me], gimme that crayon [pointing to the crayon]."

Now, being a teacher who believes that language skills are taught, I said, "My name is Mrs. Whyte. Can you think of a different way to ask me for the crayon?" The child looked at me with a really puzzled expression, so I said, "Maybe you could start with 'Mrs. Whyte, could you . . .'" The child repeated, "Mrs. Whyte, could you gimme that crayon?" I looked at him and said, "Is there anything you could add?" After a moment he said, "Now!"

This was a great child with so much potential in life who wanted desperately to say what I wanted to hear. Unfortunately, he had absolutely no idea what that was. Manners are important, and he hadn't learned them. Do we fault the child or do we accept that he doesn't know or understand what it is that we want?

I think that we should look at a situation like this one and conclude that we need to work on manners with this class. Possibly the children know their manners and are forgetting to use them, but it's also possible that they don't even know what manners are. If that's the case, the solution is to teach them.

Words That Hold Big Meaning in Our Class

We use lots of words with children that we consider to hold great meaning. It sure would be nice if the *children* understood what those words meant. If certain words hold great meaning for you (such as *empathy, kindness, please, thank you,* and *excuse me*), each word warrants a lesson that demonstrates exactly what it means and why it plays a role in your community and the world at large. Most of all, it's important for children to understand how words such as these can help them in communicating with others.

Let's say you want children to understand the word *kind*. You might use the following lessons to explain and model what *kind* means.

Day 1: Brainstorm what the word means to the children. Ask them "What does *kind* mean?" They'll respond with things such as "be nice," "share," "don't bite," "don't call people names," and "help others."

Day 2: Talk about *kind* versus *unkind*. Ask the children to give you kind responses and unkind responses to a number of situations. You might say, "There is an open chair next to you, and a friend is walking toward it to sit down. What would be a kind thing to do? What would be an unkind thing to do?"

Day 3: Ask children to identify words that are wicked. Remember to tell them that you know all the swear words, and although those are inappropriate, they're not the words you're referring to. Lead them to identify words that hurt others. They might suggest *hate, ugly, dummy, stupid,* or *shut up.* Have the children stand in a circle. Write each word on a piece of paper and give each child a word. Tell them that they won't need these words because they won't be using "wicked words" in this class. Tell each child to crumple up his paper into the smallest ball possible. Then tell them to put the balls of paper on the floor and "stamp out" the words by stepping on the balls. Have each child pass his word to the person on his right so that child can stamp out the word, too. Then kick the words into the middle of the circle. Using a broom (a witch's broom from a Halloween costume is wonderful), sweep the words into a dustpan and throw them in the garbage. Explain that now the words are gone with the trash and no one will be using them in this class.

Day 4: Role-play the difference that tone of voice can make. Give the children statements and questions and ask them to try

Don't assume that children know and understand the meaning of these words.

saying or reading the statements or questions in different tones of voice. For example, use the statement "You may share my crayons." Ask the children to read that statement in a kind tone of voice and then in a sarcastic tone of voice. You might even need to have the children echo your voice with a kind tone and then with a sarcastic tone. Many won't know the difference until they actually hear you demonstrate it.

Day 5: Choose a character you've been reading about. Ask the children to tell you whether the character is kind and why or why not. Some characters that work well for this are A. Wolf from *The True Story of the Three Little Pigs,* the Gingerbread Man, Shrek, and Angelica from the Rugrats.

This example for teaching what it means to be kind is just the beginning. Other words that hold great value to you in your classroom might include *responsible, polite, honest, reliable, fair, equal,* and *respectful.* Don't assume that children know and understand the meaning of these words. Use each word and check for understanding by asking the children what it means. If they don't have a firm understanding and it's a word that you feel is important for communication, you'll need to teach them what the word means.

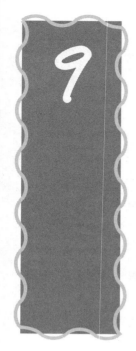

CORNERSTONE #4: COMMUNITY

You can create some thought-provoking discussions by asking teachers, "If you could have only one classroom rule, what would it be?" When I raise this question in my presentations, many teachers answer with an all-encompassing rule such as "Be respectful" (which would cover respecting others, yourself, and the class's materials). Some suggest using the Golden Rule, treating others as you would want them to treat you. Sometimes I hear "Make good choices" or "Do your best." I like all of these.

It's important to identify an "umbrella" rule that includes everything you hold most dear. My rule is "Be kind" (to yourself and others). I consider this rule to be of the utmost importance. In the previous chapter, I suggested lessons to teach the meaning of the word *kind* to children. When you create lessons to support your one rule, make sure those lessons

define the rule and include behaviors that show the rule being followed.

I've heard teachers tell children to be kind. If manners are not expected at home and kind words are not essential in sending messages in a child's home environment, where would she have learned to be kind? How would she know what that statement means? Find your own "golden rule" or "umbrella rule" and develop the standards and curriculum for the rule. Don't assume that children know what you mean. Teach them.

A good way to start is by establishing a classroom environment in which children are comfortable and safe—one where they feel that they belong and are valued. That's your community. Give them a place where they'll want to learn. You can begin with the physical surroundings.

The Physical Environment

I once heard a principal say that "children rarely misbehave in places where they want to be." I think that statement makes a lot of sense. Why would someone behave in an inappropriate manner if he wanted to stay in a particular environment? Wouldn't he do all that he could to remain in a place that's comfortable and makes him feel good?

The classrooms that are most successful in building community have some similarities. They are comfortable, cheerful, bright, and safe, and the children are involved in creating them. As a result, the children feel ownership and a sense of belonging. That's a wonderful step toward building a sense of community.

In my travels across the United States, I've seen some schools that do a wonderful job of "inviting" children to belong. These schools were built for children. The toilets are miniature, the sinks are lower, and the paper towel dispensers give out only one sheet at a time (so little people can do it themselves). The pictures are hung at waist level for an adult but at the perfect height for children. The door handles are also at child height. Each time I walk into a school that looks and feels as if it was built with children in mind, my heart is warmed to know how comfortable a child must feel entering the doors.

LITTLE CHANGES CAN MAKE A BIG DIFFERENCE

Maybe you can't change the construction of your school building, but you can make sure your classroom is welcoming to children. I've seen seemingly small physical additions to classrooms make a big difference in the emotional climate of those classrooms. Here are some ideas.

- A shelf or bookcase where children can put pictures of their families
- A couch, beanbag chairs, or rocking chairs
- Plants
- Soft lighting
- Curtains
- Chair cushions
- Individual mailboxes
- Cubbies or other assigned spaces for personal belongings
- Flowers
- Personal fans
- Classroom pets

On a sunny day, I just want to stay out there and enjoy the space.

I bet you've had the experience of entering an environment and thinking, "Wow, I love how this place makes me feel! I want to stay here." And I bet you can think back to another time when you entered an environment and thought, "How long do I have to be here? This is horrible! I can't wait to get out." Think of the amount of money and energy that has been spent setting up environments that will induce people to stay longer and feel comfortable. Some businesses are built around getting people to stay longer. Think about a casino: comfortable chairs, free drinks and meals, a bright atmosphere, and a very friendly staff entice you to stick around. In other situations, the folks who run a business might provide a couch, free coffee, a television, or magazines to make you feel comfortable.

You've probably created a space somewhere, at some time, that brings out good feelings in you. I have a deck on the back of my house that's peaceful. I can sit in a great rocking chair and watch what's going on at the bird feeder. Most of the time, I can't even hear the phone ring. On a sunny day, I just want to stay out there and enjoy the space. I feel as if I belong there. Children can gain that same feeling when we take the time to examine space and the feelings it evokes.

The Emotional Setting

The physical environment of the classroom matters, but the emotional environment is important, too. Children need to feel

All of us would like to believe that we have some control over our own destiny. Children are no different.

that the adults and other children in the classroom care about them. Do you know that old saying, "Children don't care how much you know until they know how much you care"? This statement says so much about the teaching profession. Children are told that we're the "people with the knowledge," but in many ways, knowledge is the smallest part of our interactions with children. To touch their brains, we must touch their hearts!

The classroom should be a setting in which children are empowered and expected to make choices. That means there needs to be an overall sense that children are capable human beings who can and should be actively involved in the learning process—not robots who are expected just to sit and take in information. When children don't have the chance to participate actively, then you end up with emotional and behavioral issues, and the children expect you to take charge and resolve those issues. That's so unnecessary! All of us would like to believe that we have some control over our own destiny. Children are no different. We must support them as they build skills and strategies they can use in school and in life.

One of the simplest steps to help build a sense of community is to allow the children to come up with a classroom name and/or motto. Either of these provides ownership and ties the children together. I have consistently referred to the children I work with as "Smarties," but any name that makes them feel connected to one another is good. Teams have names, businesses have names, and families have names. Why not classrooms?

Sharing a common name allows people to form a bond. In many instances, it's the first step toward unity.

Children need to feel emotionally safe in their classroom community if they're going to be willing to take risks in their learning. So often children hesitate or don't get involved for fear of being wrong, being criticized, or being laughed at. If you want children to feel safe and to succeed, you need to establish a zero-tolerance policy for bullying. This type of behavior is not acceptable in a supportive community atmosphere.

Emotional safety also involves issues such as self-esteem, positive communication, peer relationships, and handling feelings. Children who believe that they can "do it" often set themselves up for success. Building a community with a positive emotional environment can support that.

The 3 Rs: Routines, Rituals & Responsibilities

Every classroom needs routines, rituals, and a shared understanding of responsibilities to help organize and maintain order. It's essential that children know where to put their coats, what to do with papers, and what procedure they're supposed to follow for using the drinking fountain or bathroom. Each of these small items would take so much classroom time if we didn't establish routines and rituals, and so we know routines and rituals are vital. But they also matter for another, equally important reason: they allow teachers to instill a sense of responsibility in students. I've seen far too many teachers make the mistake of taking on too much responsibility for children in the early grades.

Routines Help Communities Work Together

Let's think about how children come into school and get ready for the day. The routine might look something like this:

1. Come straight to the classroom from your bus or breakfast assignment.
2. Hang up or put away any outerwear in your locker area.
3. Open your book bag and take out your home-school folder, your lunch or lunch money, and any borrowed materials.
4. Hang your book bag on the hook.
5. If you brought your lunch from home, put your lunch box or bag on the shelf. (Use the small step stool if the shelf is too high for you.)
6. If you are buying lunch, put your money in the lunch envelope in the pocket chart and add a tally mark to the board for the lunch count.
7. Return any borrowed materials (books, markers, etc.) to the appropriate place.
8. Bring your home-school folder to the greeting line.
9. Wait your turn and be ready to say good morning.
10. Get started on your morning work.

In introducing this type of routine, show children how it's similar to routines that might be in place at home. For instance, the routine for dinnertime might include setting the table, getting drinks, eating, clearing the dishes, washing the dishes, putting away leftovers, and wiping the table. Compare children's home routines to your expectations for what they should do when they get to school.

Establish routines for entering the classroom, lining up at the door, going to lunch, moving to other activities when work is finished, using the bathroom, taking drink breaks, and many

My heart would be broken if she forgot, and I think that she would feel the same way if I forgot.

other activities that occur on a regular basis. These are important components of any class, and routines need to be in place to allow things to run smoothly and efficiently. Teaching and practicing these routines is well worth the time and effort, because when routines are firmly established, not only will they save valuable classroom time but they will also build responsibility in children.

Rituals Bind Us Together

Rituals remind me of holidays, traditions, and "what we always do." They evoke positive emotions in me when I look forward to these things in my own life. My mom lives several hours from me during the summer and too many hours from me in the winter. I cherish the time we spend together, and I also cherish the good-bye ritual we go through every time we part. We stay glued eye to eye until we can no longer see each other, and in the final second before the plane, car, or camper pulls away, we blow a kiss to each other. My heart would be broken if she forgot, and I think that I can speak for her in saying that she would feel the same way if I forgot. It's our ritual, something we've done for as long as we've lived apart.

In the classroom, I want to create rituals the children look forward to. These can be things such as morning greeting, morning message, things we wear for certain events, the way we say good-bye, and any other shared actions that become part of our community and hold special meaning for us.

Ask any substitute teacher what it's like to be in a classroom in which he doesn't know the rituals.

One of our classroom rituals is to hold a morning meeting each day once all of the children are in the classroom. When we first arrive at the designated place in the room—a carpeted corner with our easel, CD player, calendar, and so on—we do some kind of morning greeting. Sometimes it's silly and sometimes it's serious, but it's always kind, and as we exchange the greeting, we're always eye to eye. The rule is to look the other person in the eye when you greet her. Greeting people is a basic social skill, learning to look someone in the eye when you're talking to her is a communication skill, and acknowledging others is good manners.

If you create classroom rituals with your students, those rituals will aid you in building a more cohesive community. You may be amazed at how excited the children are about the rituals. Ask any substitute teacher what it's like to be in a classroom in which he doesn't know the rituals. The members of the classroom community will be the first to tell him, "This is the way *we* do it." The "we" signifies their understanding that this is a group effort. Communities are support groups for their members, and working together is part of that support. Isn't this what we want for our classrooms?

Responsibility Builds Accountability

We expect everyone to show responsibility in certain ways: you're supposed to wait your turn, share the supplies, and communicate needs appropriately within the group. All of those things support the group dynamics. Many teachers also assign jobs to individual students that encourage them to be productive members of the group. The jobs are often things that benefit everyone in the community. "Paper passers," for example, ensure that everyone gets the materials the teacher needs to have passed out. They're responsible for taking care of the materials and making sure nothing is missing.

These types of jobs build accountability in children. To an adult, taking a message to the office may seem like a small thing, but assigning that errand to a child says to the child, "I trust you to be in the hall without an adult and to deliver this message to the recipient." That's huge for some children and makes them feel like an important part of the community.

Teaching Problem Solving Can Be a Group Activity

You've heard the saying "Two heads are better than one." Well, I believe that children feed off one another's ideas and words. Therefore, when problems arise that affect the entire class, the students should brainstorm solutions and decide on a course of action. This is the perfect opportunity to use communication skills, brainstorm choices, and build community with a unified plan. It's also a great way to demonstrate how a democracy works.

Here's a scenario worth thinking about: my kickball dilemma. It started out as a dictatorship issue and ended up as a problem-solving discussion in our class.

I had purchased several kickballs for the playground. Many had been lost in the past, and I wanted to ensure that our class would keep track of the balls. So I established a firm and clear rule: if *you* take the kickball out, *you* bring the kickball in. Seems easy enough, doesn't it? But we know that things are never as easy as they seem when you add in twenty-some young children. The first issue became who would take the balls out. I intervened with another rule, this time stating that there would be no arguing; the class helpers for the day would take the balls out. Issue solved—for the time being.

By the end of the week, I was beside myself with what I had witnessed involving those balls. I decided that it was time for a meeting of the minds. I gathered the children on the carpet and let them know how I felt. I said I had bought the balls in hopes of adding joy to the playground, and now they had become a nightmare for me. I told the children that each day, when it was time to line up after recess, I'd watched as they yanked balls from each other's hands and took them to the line. I'd watched

One of the quietest boys in the class raised his hand and said, "Mrs. Whyte, I think this is your fault."

as the children the balls had been taken from whined and cried and screamed. I'd watched children give other children dirty looks when they got in line to go inside. I told them I felt frustrated and disappointed in them. I had decided that I was taking the balls away and no one would get to play with them.

One of the quietest boys in the class raised his hand and said, "Mrs. Whyte, I think this is your fault." I was stunned. "My fault? I don't grab the ball from other people on the playground," I told him. He answered, "But you made the rule, and the rule doesn't work."

When I asked him to explain, he reminded me that the rule was that whoever took the ball out was supposed to bring the ball in. "That makes problems," he said, "when the person who takes the ball out doesn't play with it or finishes playing with it and leaves it with someone else. Then the bell rings or the flag waves, and that person knows they're responsible for bringing the ball in, so they go and get it. That's not always easy because some of the kids want to finish what they're doing before they get in line. One time I didn't even see the flag, and someone came and grabbed the ball I was playing with. That's what makes people upset."

Other children started to chime in about times when this had happened to them. Finally, I felt the need to regroup, so I asked the children what they thought a solution to this problem might be. One said that whoever has the ball when she sees the flag or hears the bell should bring it in. I asked, "What if no one is

We didn't lose any balls that year, and there wasn't any more fighting over them. Lesson learned: teacher doesn't always know best!

playing with it at the time? Won't it get left outside?" They considered that, and another child offered this solution: whoever brought the ball outside could be the "ball checker," to be sure that someone in line has the ball. That person doesn't have to carry it, just see that it's there. If the checker doesn't see the ball, it should be his job to find it.

My head was spinning, so I talked out the plan with the children. "Let me get this straight," I told them. "The helpers will take the balls out. Whoever has a ball when it's time to come in will bring the ball to the line, and the helpers will check to be sure the balls are coming back inside." One student said, "You can help by reminding the helpers to check for the ball that's the same color as the one they brought out." Finally, I said, "Let me think this through. Do you all think this will work and will end the problem of fighting over the balls?" They were in agreement.

We put their problem-solving abilities to the test the next day. We didn't lose any balls that year, and there wasn't any more fighting over them. Lesson learned: teacher doesn't always know best!

Stress & the Classroom

Even when no kickballs are involved, communities tend to be places with lots of action. There are always multiple things going on that involve lots of different people. At times this can be very stressful for young children (and their teachers). It's imperative to the success of any community that we learn to recognize symptoms of stress and find ways to manage it.

Lots of different emotions can cause individuals to feel stressed. Fear, apprehension, moodiness, anger, frustration, and uncertainty are a few of the emotions that signal stress attacks. Sometimes we see similar problems when we're overtired or overwhelmed and just plain feel like there's too much on our plates. This can lead to some of the physical signs of stress: headaches, stomachaches, the inability to sleep or eat, the inability to pay attention, acting out, crying, screaming, or being physically out of control.

Recognizing that life is stressful is the first step toward dealing with the emotions and symptoms that accompany stress. It's been said that half the problem is recognizing that you have a problem. When stress is identified in young children, adults should look for the source of the stress and know what actions they can or cannot take to reduce or relieve it. Sometimes you can support a child and reduce her stress level by talking with her, acknowledging her feelings, and brainstorming choices. Have you ever thought that you felt better after talking a problem out with someone? Children don't always have the words to express what's bothering them, so it's important to teach them to communicate how they feel and to acknowledge what they can and can't do about those feelings.

I once read an article on stress that noted how sometimes just dropping something from a hectic schedule can do wonders for reducing stress. Some children need our help in identifying when too much is happening. Others just need to learn to relax, and that's hard for children who go from 0 to 90 in five seconds flat. Many times I tell children to breathe, and they say, "I can't." What they don't realize is that they're already breathing, but if they learn to take deep breaths and to focus on their breathing pattern, they can reduce stress. Exercise can reduce stress, too, and exercise can include a nice walk around the school building. Solutions to stress don't have to be complicated; the whole point is to make things less overwhelming.

It seems to me that some of the most stressful situations for young children come from change. Change is hard for everyone. It never seems to matter whether the change is good, bad, or indifferent; it still causes stress. We are creatures of habit, and learning to deal with change is always tough. Talk through changes and go slowly with young children. Those simple steps may make a world of difference in their stress levels.

Tolerance Is Taught, Modeled & Expected

A common source of stress in classrooms is the perception, "That's not fair!" But what does *fair* mean? One definition might be "free from bias or injustice." Does *fair* mean *equal*? Is there ever a time when treating someone fairly doesn't mean treating that person the same way you're treating the rest of the group? This happens every day in real life. People are treated fairly, but that doesn't necessarily mean they're all treated the same.

My belief has always been that you treat each child fairly according to his academic, behavioral, and emotional needs. It amazes me that anyone could really believe that to treat all children equally would in any way be fair. If one child needs a step stool to reach the shelf where his lunch box goes, it's not unfair to let him use the step stool. It's unequal, because other children may not need the step stool, but it's certainly not unfair. We

"I understand that, Mrs. Whyte, but we know that _____ needs a little bit more understanding."

want children to learn tolerance for differences; those differences should not be ignored but instead should be acknowledged and accepted.

It's amazing to me how often children recognize what other children need. I remember a time when a child in one of my classes came to the defense of a student who had been reprimanded in the cafeteria. She felt that the way the monitor had talked to this child had escalated the situation until the child acted out in an inappropriate way. I told her the monitor had been enforcing a rule that applied to everyone. The child said, "I understand that, Mrs. Whyte, but we know that _____ needs a little bit more understanding than some of us." I loved seeing in her face the understanding that coping with directions was more difficult for this child than for most. Perhaps we could learn a lot from children who respond like this.

Adults are the role models for tolerance and acceptance. We should be very cautious in the words and actions we choose, as children will follow our lead. When a child questions why another child might be treated a certain way, I always say, "Each of us needs to figure out who's the most important person to them in this classroom. Be concerned with how the most important person is treated and decide if that's fair." I love working with young children; whenever I say to worry about the most important person in the classroom, they always say, "That's *you*." I often have to explain, "No, not me. *You* are the most important person to yourself, so focus your energy on yourself."

Rewards for All

It's important to expose children to intangible rewards as well as tangible ones. If you'd like to provide rewards that are based on helping children to "feel good" when they make good choices, you might consider some of the following.

Notes to Students

One of my favorite rewards is the simple thank-you or acknowledgment note. Have you ever received a thank-you note that you didn't expect? What a great feeling it is to know that someone noticed something you did and took the time to write and let you know. Recipients often save these types of notes because they leave a warm feeling of being appreciated.

I want children to know that I appreciate it when they make good choices, when they go out of their way to do something nice, or when they simply make life easier for others by being good people. Take the time to write a note to say "thank you" or "I noticed" and place it in a spot where the child will find it. You could put it in a cubby, on a desk, or between the pages of a journal. I love the smile that spreads over a child's face when she finds a note from me letting her know that she's appreciated for the things she does and the person she is.

Notes Home

How often do you send home a note about the "good stuff"? Most of us have had to write the dreaded note to parents outlining what a child did wrong. Most of these notes define behaviors we consider inappropriate. How many of us set up our communities to share the good as well as the bad?

I love the smile that spreads over a child's face when she finds a note from me letting her know that she's appreciated.

If you take the time to write a line or two on a postcard letting parents know what you appreciate about their child, and if you continue to do that on a regular basis, you can build a bridge that will weather many a storm. It's hard to be a parent who consistently hears the bad. Find the good in every child and celebrate it in writing. Doing that will remind you, the parents, and the child that although things can be rough at times, there's a good person inside.

I like to have postcards with address labels and stamps ready to go each month. Then I can choose four or five children a week and think of a positive comment to share about each one. I send the cards in the mail and often reap the benefits of being a "bearer of good news."

Time with the Teacher

I don't know many children who wouldn't love to spend more time with their teachers. A reward for being a kind person who's an asset to the community can be for the child to have lunch with the teacher on a particular day of the week. You may not eat lunch with every child every single week, but don't forget to let everyone know that not being included is a natural consequence of choices they've made. I tell my students I like to eat lunch with children who show respect for themselves and others, who take turns talking, and who follow the rules. Let the children know why they're chosen to be lunch buddies. In real life, we choose to eat with people we want to spend time with.

I let the children know that any week, they can choose to be that kind of person.

Book Choice

Children who enjoy books will feel rewarded when they're offered an opportunity to borrow a book. Let students know that you have certain books that are reserved for children you trust to follow the rules.

Free Pass

Identify times when a child can earn a free pass to do something she enjoys (such as taking a special journal bag home) or to avoid something he would rather not do (such as homework). It feels good to be rewarded in this way.

Borrowing a Pet or a Stuffed Animal

A reward that children adore is to be responsible for the class pet. Make sure they know that to earn this reward, they need to be responsible and trustworthy.

Special Chair, Cushion, or Desk

Children also love to be rewarded with time in a special place. If children consistently do what I ask them to do and are responsible and kind in our community, I might reward them with a chance to sit in a special place for a specific time (such as during Morning Meeting). Children love this acknowledgment that they've been on task.

Personal Music Setup

A personal music setup (including earphones!) makes a great reward. I tape songs that children like and let them listen to the

I like knowing that if I pay attention to my work and get it done, then I get to play hard.

music at their desks during different times of the day. It's a special treat.

Sharing Recess with Another Class

What a great feeling it is to earn the right to "goof off" with other people whose company you enjoy. It's certainly one of my favorite rewards in life. I like knowing that if I pay attention to my work and get it done, then I get to play hard. This is something my students enjoy as well.

Game Hour

Offer children who have worked hard all week the option to play games for an hour. Children who have not done their work can use this time to catch up. Be careful to distinguish between children who *purposely* don't do their work when given time and those who just aren't able to finish their work in the given time. I often reward children who I feel have done their absolute best to stay on task but were not able to finish everything. We can't all do the same thing in the same amount of time.

Other Special Treats

Treats come in many forms. Maybe a child gets to do his math problems on the sidewalk with colored chalk. Maybe he gets extra recess time. Bubble wands with bubble mix are often a huge success. Be creative when you think of rewards and treats for your class.

I once came to class as Old Mother Hubbard to read silly rhymes. The children were all ears.

A Special Reader

It's nice to tell children that you're so proud of who they are and how they behave that you've invited a special guest to read in your class. An older sibling of one of the students is always a big hit. If you don't find someone from outside the class, become a special reader yourself by dressing up in a costume. I once came to class as Old Mother Hubbard to read silly rhymes. The children were all ears for the "special reader," even though they knew it was me.

Warm Fuzzies

A pom-pom with googly eyes and a fuzzy nose—what my students and I call a "Snookle"—is a sweet symbol of a "warm fuzzy." You can hot-glue one to a clothespin or stick a pin back to it, allowing a child to wear it. I share Snookles when I want individual children to be recognized for giving warm fuzzies to me or other members of our community.

Slipper, Hat, Sock, or PJ Day

Allow a class that follows the rules to break the rules now and then. Tell them to wear slippers, special socks, hats, or pj's to school. It can be a fun writing activity to have students ask the principal's permission to break the rules. Tell them to justify their position—for example, why they should be allowed to wear slippers for a day. If the writing campaign is successful and you get permission, encourage the principal and office staff to join in.

Sharing Time

One of the most effective rewards I know is to publicly acknowledge and show appreciation for children who show self-control, are kind to others, and are responsible members of the classroom community. Have the children sit in a circle, then talk with them. Begin with a statement such as one of the following:

- I appreciate _____ because . . .
- I like it when I see/hear that _____ has . . .
- Something I value about having _____ in our classroom is . . .
- I noticed something that _____ did/said, and I wanted to say thank you.

Think of your own life. How does it feel to be acknowledged for the things you do and say that others appreciate? I also have another goal during this time: to model for children how to let others know how they feel, how to share positive comments, and how to respond when people take notice. One of the hardest things to teach children is how to accept a compliment. In fact, I'm sure you know many adults who have trouble with the concept of being complimented. We should demonstrate to children that it's all right to feel full of pride when someone takes notice of them.

Building & Understanding Community

Before children go to school, the main exposure many have to "community" is within their own households. That's good; it means they have some experience in getting along with others and working together. But household communities usually involve fewer children and more adults than classroom communities. That means it can be a challenge getting children to think of their classroom as a community. It can also be an opportunity. Classrooms must become communities so that all of the children learn to get along and to help, and be helped by, others. Let's be sure we acknowledge the challenge and prepare children to learn more by learning together.

You Catch More Flies with Honey Than with Vinegar

I will believe this old saying until the day I leave this earth. My goal is to act on it constantly because I have seen the truth of it in working with people. Vinegar (demanding, not appreciating, or just being "short") rarely works as well as honey (asking politely, showing appreciation, and being genuine). Model this for children. Always be someone who believes that being kind and polite is much more powerful than being rude and demanding.

Members of Communities Help One Another

Teaching children to lend a hand or jump in when someone needs help is important in a community in which people care about one another. Ask the children in your class to think of how they could help someone in a range of situations, such as the following:

- Someone loses someone or something that means a great deal to her.
- Someone trips on the way to the bus, and the contents of his backpack spill out onto the sidewalk.
- Someone forgets her book at home and has nothing to read during reading time.

Tell them that we are all going to fit together in this class, but we must first figure out how.

- Someone calls a classmate a name, and it hurts that child's feelings.
- Someone has his hands full with heavy items and needs to open a door.

These are everyday situations in which we have the power to make someone's day a little better. Teach children to be willing to help and to be ready to appreciate it when someone helps them. This will make for a successful community.

Everyone Fits In

A fun activity for building community in the classroom is to cut up a large piece of butcher paper into puzzle pieces and give each child one piece. Tell them that we are all going to fit together in this class, but we must first figure out how. Ask one child at a time to come forward with his puzzle piece and see if he can figure out where it might fit. Eventually, the pieces will begin to match up. Continue until all the pieces are in place. Then tape the pieces together and ask each child to draw herself on any puzzle piece she chooses within the community. Encourage students to let their drawings overlap onto neighboring pieces to emphasize the concept of community. Hang the finished puzzle on display.

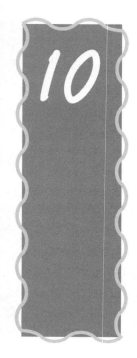

The Toolbox of Management Techniques

The four cornerstones of positive discipline—self-control, choice, communication, and community—are the starting points for building a positive classroom environment. These cornerstones require you to work with all of your students to establish a classroom in which these four ideals are respected

and valued. Of course, we all know there will be times when this overall approach is not what we need to deal with an individual child at a particular time. So in this chapter, let's address some specific issues that we face in classrooms every day. Let's look at what we can do to address those issues before problems come up. And since experience has taught us that there will be times when we'll need to react to off-target behaviors, let's also talk about how we can plan for those times.

Only you can decide which of these techniques will work with your teaching style, your philosophy, your personality, and the children you're teaching in any given situation and any given year. It is my hope that you'll find several that you can add to your management toolbox and pull out when they're needed. As you try any or all of them, please keep one rule in mind: if one strategy isn't working, move on and try something else.

Keeping the Focus of the Group

Often management issues arise when children aren't paying attention or are bored. This can happen with an entire class. When the students are acting uninterested or are beginning to daydream during whole-group lessons, it may be time to refocus them. What are our options when we're "losing them"?

Use Humor

Make them giggle, and you'll get their attention back. Be silly, tell a joke, and acknowledge that everyone needs a break now and then. Often we become serious or act put out when children are not paying attention, but this can actually escalate the problem. Sometimes your best recourse might be to lighten things up.

I have a pretend "noisemometer" for when the class is too loud. I tell them that the temperature is going up and the voices

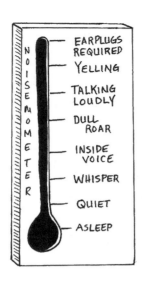

NOISEMOMETER

— EARPLUGS REQUIRED
— YELLING
— TALKING LOUDLY
— DULL ROAR
— INSIDE VOICE
— WHISPER
— QUIET
— ASLEEP

need to go down. You can also use a puppet to model being a ventriloquist when children are talking for other children. Tell them you don't want anyone being a ventriloquist for another child; only puppets like it when somebody else talks for them.

Several years ago, I worked with a teacher who hung up a picture of the president in her classroom and told her students that any tattling should be referred to the most important person in the room. She explained that they should "tell it to the president." This is one more form of humor that might aid you in refocusing the class.

I use humor in another situation, too. Each year a simple rule is stated in classrooms across our country: "Leave toys and important items at home. They don't belong at school." And each year this rule is broken in every classroom. Therefore, I keep a lockbox for such occasions. I explain that there are items that don't belong at school, and I tell the child that to keep her belonging safe, I'll need to put it in the box under lock and key. Sometimes I return the item at the end of the day, and other times I ask a parent to stop by to pick it up at their convenience.

This is a lighthearted way to handle what's become an ongoing struggle for many teachers. You can reduce the power struggle of taking treasured belongings from children—and keep the focus on learning—if you have a plan for what will happen if they choose to bring those treasures to school.

Change the Pace

Sometimes all you need to do to regain children's attention is to change the pace. Know when to let go of a lesson that's going nowhere! It may be that things are moving too slowly and you need to step up the pace a bit. Look for opportunities to change

Tell them that *listen* and *silent* have the same letters. You have to be silent to be a good listener.

your tone of voice, add hand movements, or find some other way to add energy and heighten interest in the lesson.

Show It!

Talking and showing can increase a child's ability to learn, and anytime we add a form of illustration, our chances of getting children's attention rises. If your voice is not holding their attention, it might be time to add a visual. How many times have you thought, "If only I could see it, I would probably understand"? Many of us can hear something a hundred times and not get it, but show us a picture or an example, and poof, it magically becomes clear.

Problem Solve with Cooperative Groups

At times it seems that children are just tired of the "sit and listen" method of teaching. As often as possible, we need to place them in small groups where they can talk more and listen better. This is how they will develop the best speaking skills. Learning to cooperate, take turns talking, and not monopolize the conversation will serve children well in their school years and later in life. Tell them that *listen* and *silent* have the same letters. You have to be silent to be a good listener.

Small groups are good places for practicing the skill of "agreeing to disagree." Many times we each have our own ideas and ways that we'd like to do something. That's where negoti-

There are times when all it takes to reengage children is to let them move.

ating and communication skills come into play. If children are going to learn these skills, they must be given opportunities to practice them in real situations. There's nothing quite like a group of young problem solvers. Their ideas and reactions to one another often serve to remind us how young they really are in the big scheme of life.

Summarize Key Points with Visuals

Sometimes we lose children's focus because we try to convey too much information. Remember to summarize so that children don't feel overwhelmed and let their minds drift off. Graphic organizers are a wonderful way to take massive amounts of information and categorize it for better recall. Brains like organization. When children have ways to sort and file all their new skills and information, they learn at a higher level.

Add an Activity

Move, sing, or play a game. There are times when all it takes to reengage children is to let them move or participate in an activity. When you find ways to add movement to the school day, you keep children focused and allow many kinesthetic learners to flourish. Songs can be wonderful for keeping children focused, too. I had a classroom of first graders who could list all the presidents in order. Many parents and colleagues considered this a great feat, but I had never made the children memorize a list of presidents. They were able to recall the names because they had learned them in a song; the mnemonic associations helped them to remember.

Wiggle, Giggle, or Gross Them Out!

If you really need all eyes on you, wiggle, giggle, or say something "gross." When all else fails, any of these three things tends to get students' attention. Try yelling "underwear" or "booger." It's amazing how interesting these words are to young children and how quickly they'll refocus their attention back where you want it: on you!

Helping Individuals Who Struggle to Stay on Task

Although some of these strategies can readily be used to focus all children, there is a difference between trying to refocus an entire class and supporting individual children who struggle to stay on task. Let's look at strategies that can be used with groups or individual children.

Set Aside Talk Time

In the communication chapter, we discussed how important it is to set aside a time when students can contribute to class discussions. Now let's look at another aspect of "talk time." Children are going to talk. You can add talk time to your day and structure that time, or you can expect that children will talk whenever they want; you decide. Simply allowing children the opportunity to visit with one another can be a great management technique. When children know that they'll have a chance to socialize, they're less likely to demand to do that at inappropriate times. When they're asked to return to a task after they've had their social time, they often get back to work more quickly and with less resistance.

Take a Break

We all need breaks, but we often need them at different times and for different reasons. Learning to judge which children need

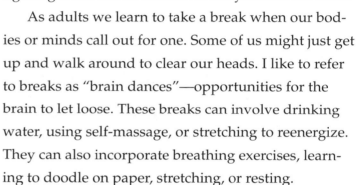

what and when is always a challenge for a teacher, but figuring it out can be a lifesaver for you and the child.

As adults we learn to take a break when our bodies or minds call out for one. Some of us might just get up and walk around to clear our heads. I like to refer to breaks as "brain dances"—opportunities for the brain to let loose. These breaks can involve drinking water, using self-massage, or stretching to reenergize. They can also incorporate breathing exercises, learning to doodle on paper, stretching, or resting.

But children need to learn acceptable ways to take a break without abusing the system. Sometimes you need to address abuse by taking some time to talk honestly about how breaks help us to maintain our focus. Reteach the techniques you've already introduced and emphasize good choices and bad choices. In the end, if children aren't able to manage their own breaks, you may need to manage their breaks for them. But do be sure to include breaks during any work time, and sometimes during playtime too.

Plan Alternative Activities

So much of what we ask children to do in school limits their creativity and fascination with a subject. There may be times when your best recourse is to ditch the familiar and allow a

Try cutting a three-part display board in half and setting it on the child's desk to create "office space."

child to complete an alternative activity to gain the skill or show proficiency. Sometimes it may be necessary to eliminate part of the work in an attempt to get at least some of it done. Crossing every other problem off a math work sheet can put a child at ease and allow him to finish the rest. Allowing a child to paint the life cycle of a butterfly instead of writing down the stages may allow her to show new skills.

Minimize Distractions

I'm an adult, and *I* am easily distracted. For children who have the same problem, it can be a huge issue. Think of a child who appears to spend a lot of time watching others and staring into space. It may be that focusing is difficult for that child unless you can eliminate distractions. Try cutting a three-part display board in half and setting it on the child's desk to create "office space." This can do wonders for a child who's easily distracted. You may be able to help a child who tends to "hear everything" by allowing her to wear noise-reduction headphones or play quiet music on a personal CD or tape player. If you recognize that some children are more easily distracted than others and look for ways to minimize the distractions, you'll go a long way toward allowing them to succeed.

Establish Visual Cues or Signals

Create visual cues or signals that individual children understand. Tell the child that the two of you will have a signal that is

Very small signals can make a big difference for children who thrive on being noticed.

a "code." This works well, for example, with a child who focuses so strongly on what she's finished that she can't seem to move on to the next step until you've checked her work. For a child like this, you might try creating a tent-style card that has two different-colored sides. Explain to the child that one color means "I need help" and the other color means "Please check this out." It's not necessary for the entire class to understand this special signal as long as the child who needs the signal understands what it means.

There's a difference between needing help to stay on task and asking for a quick check of what's been done. Let the child know that "I need help" will alert you to come as soon as possible, but that when the "Please check this out" side is showing, you expect her to continue to work on something else until you have a chance to come over. It's amazing to see how very small signals, such as a thumbs-up, can make a big difference for children who thrive on being noticed.

Address Individual Interests

It seems obvious, but when you incorporate a child's special interests in the learning process, you engage that child. A student who loves dinosaurs may be more motivated to write if you let her use stationery decorated with dinosaurs. A child who loves race cars may be more motivated to work on his math skills if you let him work out the problems with a pencil that has a car eraser on top.

Provide Background Music

Washing dishes seems like less of a chore when I'm listening to my favorite songs. I enjoy yard work more when I have the CD player outside with me playing classical music. Is it possible that some children would be calmer and more focused with music playing in the classroom? Some students may find soft background music a good way to reduce stress while they work. If other students find the music distracting, you can give them noise-reduction headsets to wear while you play the music.

Introduce Rocking Chairs

A parent once asked me how I would handle her daughter, who "just couldn't sit still." I could relate to the problem, because I was a "bouncer" as a child. (If you were a child who "bounced," you know what I'm referring to: a child who sits on a piece of furniture such as a sofa or chair and bounces against the back.) I was in constant motion, even when the assigned task was to sit still. I broke the springs and backs of several couches over the years by bouncing.

We can help young bouncers by replacing their stationary chairs with rocking chairs. If that's not possible, we can at least recognize that a bouncing motion often comforts a child who craves movement. I approached the case of the student who "just couldn't sit still" by giving her options: she could sit in her chair (even if she bounced lightly against the back); she could move the chair out of her space and rock on her legs or knees; or she could use a rocking chair. This small accommodation allowed her to stay on task.

Some teachers might say that this option isn't fair to the other children. I challenge that by saying, "It's not *equal* treatment, but it can still be fair." One of my favorite stories involves a child who said to me, "If *she* doesn't have to sit in a chair, *I* shouldn't have to." I told him, "You don't have to. I'd be glad to let you stand also." That lasted about twenty minutes before he asked for his chair back.

Children need accommodations that allow them to learn. Often what works for one child would never work for another. There are no rights or wrongs in these situations; the goal is to find a solution that works. If you offer an accommodation to one child and another child would like to try it, let him. You may be surprised at how quickly the child decides "that's not for me."

Use Space Tape

Have you ever thought, "I just need this child to stay in his space [or stay out of mine] for a bit"? If you designate space and set up the parameters for leaving or entering that space, you can manage this. I tell children that the area within the tape around their desks is "their" space, and they may use it in any way they want that keeps them working. Some lie on the floor; some sit under their desks. As long as they get their work done without distracting others, I can live with them being out of their seats.

A child said, "If *she* doesn't have to sit in a chair, *I* shouldn't have to." I told him, "I'd be glad to let you stand also." That lasted about twenty minutes.

Teach Timing

Many young children are baffled when we set time limits that have no meaning to them. The math standards in many of our states mandate that we teach children basic concepts of time: what it is, how it's measured, and how to keep track of it. If we're expected to teach these things, it doesn't make sense to assume that children have already mastered them.

Individual children vary in their ability to understand time limits. You may need to give a child a personal timer, provide a picture or model of a clock that represents the "finishing time," or just keep checking on the child at regular intervals. Always explain the concept of time to the child when you check on her, so that she can begin to internalize a concept that is still foreign to many adults: where does the time go?

Avoid Environmental Disasters

Sometimes we create the very distractions that we want to eliminate. I once asked a teacher why an easily distracted child was seated next to the door to the hallway. (By the way, there was a window in the door that was at desk height, allowing the child to watch everything going on in the hall.) She answered that he had chosen the seat. In this instance, it seemed that the child had made a bad choice: he was easily distracted and had chosen to put himself in a busy place. This was a time when the teacher needed to intervene and reassess whether the child could handle the seat he'd chosen.

In another classroom, I witnessed children constantly spinning a book carousel every time they passed it. I listened as the teacher reprimanded them and reminded them over and over not to do this. I began to wonder whether the carousel was more trouble than it was worth. Then one day when the teacher and I were conversing after school, *I* absentmindedly began to twirl the carousel. Is it possible that some things are just too tempting or that they invite interaction?

If something in your classroom needs to be off-limits to the children, you need to explain that rule to them. If it's important, you need to reiterate the rule. But many defiant children are intrigued when things are described as off-limits. I sometimes feel that we might as well just dare these children to touch those things! It's important to keep the teacher's sanity, too, so at some point, you might need to ask yourself whether it would be easier to remove the distraction either for a short time or for good.

Organizational Skills & Tools

Many problems arise when children can't seem to get organized and stay organized. We can help by teaching these skills and giving children lots of chances to practice them. For the first month of school, you may need to visit and revisit how desks, backpacks, pencil caddies, and so on are organized. If organization is an issue, design a curriculum to aid children in mastering organizational skills.

Pencil Problems

You can also address specific issues by providing a child with options. Do you have pencil problems in your classroom?

Prioritizing is a skill, and some young children don't have it.

It's hard to believe the amount of anguish teachers have suffered because of those yellow sticks with erasers on top. Whether they're lost, chewed on, used as rubber-band launchers, or broken, pencils and their issues have eaten up a lot of valuable instruction time over the years.

Let's say you want to provide options for the child who seems to be on a constant march to and from the pencil sharpener. You might tell him that he can sharpen three pencils before he sits down to work. If all three end up dull or broken during work time, he may borrow the portable mini-sharpener. If he doesn't make good choices about when he really needs the sharpener, you'll need to decide for him. (I've found that an alternative solution is to give the child a mechanical pencil.)

The "To Do" List

Tools that allow children to learn organizational skills benefit both the children and the teacher. Take a look at an individual child and ask yourself, "How can I ensure that this child stays on task today?" Perhaps you can help the child by giving her a task card that outlines exactly what she needs to do, in the order she needs to do it. Prioritizing is a skill, and some young children don't have it. Create a list and discuss why some things are more important than others and how we decide what to do first, how long to spend on that task, and when it's time to move on to the next one.

"I'm Done . . . What Should I Do Now?"

A common issue in classrooms today concerns what to do with early finishers. I happen to think that any solutions to this dilemma should also address what to do with late finishers. Here are some thoughts.

I once had a student who always finished early and was out of his seat. The biggest problem was my own aggravation that he not only did the work quickly but also did it well! As a teacher, I needed to look at this child and ask, "What else does he need from me? What other activities can I provide for him that will lead to an enriching classroom experience?"

What can children do in your class when they've finished an assignment and others need more time? Some of the traditional choices include checking their work, reading a book, cleaning and straightening their desks, or taking a nap. I think back to teachers who offered me choices like those when I was a child, and I wonder, "What were those teachers thinking? Why didn't they just ask me to look for ways to be a nuisance or off task?"

There has not been a single year that I've been in a classroom when some children didn't finish before others. This is not new; it's always been this way. Therefore, I think it's important to come up with a plan for this situation (before it arises), put the plan into play, and assess how it works. What are some options that children might actually like to try when they have some extra time—things that can also be considered learning activities? Here are a few ideas.

The Writing Box

Create a "writing box" that allows children to write for authentic reasons. Maybe they write notes, create lists, make books, or write articles. These types of writing activities tend to engage children at a higher level than the same old paperwork. Keep the box interesting by adding envelopes, stamps, different kinds of writing paper, and multiple writing utensils.

Help a Friend

Some children are natural helpers who love to assist others in the class. Never let a child take over another child's work, but do nurture the children who like to help and show them how best to help another child. Provide guidelines that teach children the role of helper.

Puzzles

Puzzles help children see things in more dimensions. They also build skills in vocabulary, visual discrimination, logical thinking, recognition, planning, associating, and so on. Give children opportunities to work with many different forms of puzzles: board puzzles, crosswords, search and finds, Sudoku puzzles, and any others that will engage them.

Computers

Depending on who you talk to, computers are the biggest blessing or the biggest curse of the century. I accept the criticisms I hear about computers, but I also accept the fact that technology isn't going away anytime soon. Let your early finishers work with the many great Web sites that provide wonderful interactive reading programs. Or let them explore the many opportunities to connect with classrooms all over the world. Use this tool and this time to let children explore learning opportunities that don't fit neatly into the scheduled curriculum.

Crayons, Beads, or Clay

When I was a child, I knew that every year I would find under the Christmas tree new crayons and coloring books. I loved to color as a child, and as an adult I worry that this is becoming a lost art form. It can be relaxing and rewarding to add color to a picture. Encourage your students to color by modeling the value of adding color to an image, by showing enthusiasm for the activity, and by sharing the excitement of color in our world.

Stringing beads, making patterns, and creating objects are all valuable skills. "Ironing beads" were one of the best options I ever came up with for my early finishers. These are the cylindrical beads that you put into pattern plates to create an image. After the image is finished, you iron it (that's where an adult comes in) to melt the beads and form a finished project. The end results make great magnets, necklaces, and so on. Even better, children spend days quietly working on these creations. These beads are available in many craft stores and in the craft sections of large department stores. They seem to hold a hypnotic appeal for the young, and they're also great for building dexterity and motor skills.

Clay has a similar attraction. I believe it should be a permanent fixture in every classroom for young students. Many children are entertained by rolling and molding clay, and its artistic value can't be denied.

Some people feel that classrooms shouldn't provide fun activities because children will prefer those and will want to get to them.

What's the Rush?

At this point, you may be wondering what to do about those children who rush through their work to get to these activities. That's always a concern. Some people feel that classrooms shouldn't provide fun activities because children will prefer those and will want to get to them quickly. For those who feel that way, here are some questions that I hope will be food for thought: Don't we want children to be motivated to finish their work in a timely fashion? Aren't *you* more motivated to finish work that's not very interesting to you when you know that something fun is waiting for you? What would happen if we all rushed through our work to get to the fun stuff? Would that create problems? Would our work suffer?

Address this problem with your students ahead of time. Explain the goal of the extra activities, and tell students when they'll have the chance to try them. Show empathy with their desire to get to the fun stuff quickly, but outline why that won't be a good choice in the end. If you consistently see a child making bad choices, it's your job to intervene and help the child explore good choices. Children need to know that if they choose to rush and not complete work or do their best, the teacher will decide when they're able to participate and which activity choices will be available.

Reiterate that it all comes down to choices. Make good choices, and you'll get to make your own. Consistently make poor choices, and the teacher will need to intervene. Don't give

Fun activities motivate; boring activities lead to management issues. That's *your* choice.

up on your students. Regroup, reteach, and expect that they'll learn. Remember, fun activities motivate; boring activities lead to management issues. That's *your* choice.

We All Work at Different Speeds

An important side note to this topic concerns the children who never finish early and never get to try the things that seem to be more fun. I worry most about these children. If the fun things in education drive motivation, it's imperative that all children experience these things. This may mean that once in a while, you need to eliminate some of the "must do" work in order to allow time for choice activities. Maybe you'll need to evaluate what you're asking of a child, or maybe you'll need to build the child's motivation to finish her required work. Whatever the situation, every child in your class should be able to finish her assignments and then choose activities that promote learning and provide a break from more traditional classroom work.

Addressing Difficult Behaviors

Now it's time to turn to some of the more difficult behavior issues teachers face—things such as constant interruptions, defiant actions, uncooperative attitudes, and breaking the rules. What tools can we use to incorporate the four cornerstones of discipline and deal effectively with these issues? Here are some possibilities you may want to consider adding to your toolbox.

Self-Evaluation

Often we tell children what *we* don't like or value in their behavior. But it's also important to ask them to evaluate their own actions and words. After all, would you be motivated to change your behavior if you didn't see anything wrong with it?

Self-evaluation can be written or oral, private or public. Whatever the format, the evaluation must give the child a chance to examine and evaluate the behavior from her point of view. Many times we want to jump in and give children our version before we hear them out. Children need to know that they're heard and understood. This goes back to the issue of empathy: we don't have to agree with their evaluation, but we do have to acknowledge it. Then we need to ask the child to really think about the behavior, the motivation or feelings behind the behavior, and what might be a more appropriate response to a similar situation in the future.

Meeting with Myself

We addressed the strategy of time-out in the communication chapter, but time-out is also a stand-alone management option. There are times when it's necessary to convey to a child that you need time to think or that you feel that the child needs time to assess something that's happened. Direct the child to a predetermined quiet space that's available for students to meet with themselves. Time is a gift, not a punishment. Often the gift of time leads to solutions that work. This strategy should be firmly established as a *positive* alternative to escalating emotions so that when it's needed, it's perceived in a positive manner.

Some children respond well to having a written plan and signing on the dotted line.

Planned Ignoring

Never underestimate the power of taking away an audience. Children who thrive on negative attention will do anything to have a stage. If they believe that they have no audience, sometimes the behavior de-escalates fairly quickly.

Direct Appeal

There are times when a direct appeal is the simplest and most effective way to handle a situation. Use your classroom communication skills. Remember to talk *with* children, not at them. Or use "I . . ." or "You . . ." statements. Making a statement such as "I need you to stop what you're doing" just might do the trick.

Negotiate a Contract

Some children respond well to having a written plan and then committing to it by signing on the dotted line. The contract states the problem, what can be done to solve it, the student's choice of what he will do (if there's more than one option), and when the commitment will be honored. The contract also should outline the consequences if the student doesn't follow through. This is a formal agreement between two parties, and it should be known that each party has committed to it. This approach spotlights the problem, possible solutions, and a commitment to the future.

Reinforce the Positive

We addressed "rewards for all" in the chapter on community, and many of those same rewards work well with individual children. This definitely includes those who've been labeled as "troublemakers." Catch them being good and catch them often. Praise is one of the best motivators to make good choices in the future. In your classroom, do people spend as much time noticing the good as they do addressing the bad?

Two Weeks, Two Minutes a Day

When a child's behavior is a constant concern, your best solution may be a proactive, prolonged approach. Remember, when emotions are high, problem solving is low. Make a commitment that you'll meet with the child each and every day for two weeks. If you know that you will need to be out of the class for one or more days, try to hold off on using the strategy until you can commit to the full two weeks.

Each day of the two weeks, spend two uninterrupted minutes with the child, one-on-one. If you don't have another adult in your classroom, it may be that the only time you'll be able to do this will be when you take the class to an outside activity such as lunch. Send all the children in to the activity except the one you need to talk to; ask that child to remain in the hall for a moment. Don't make this sound like a punishment, but instead say it in a way that invites the child to spend a couple of minutes with you. You might say, "Connor, can you please stay with me for a moment?"

As soon as you're alone with him, get down to his level (remember, this is personal). Touch his hand or shoulder (if it's okay with him) and state the facts. You might say, "Connor,

"What do you think you or I could do differently so that this doesn't happen again?"

you and I are having a rough time. This morning when I asked you to pay attention in Morning Meeting, you kept on fooling around. This behavior makes it hard for me to teach. Can you understand that? What do you think you or I could do differently so that this doesn't happen again?" You're addressing the behavior when it's not occurring, which makes it less likely that he'll feel threatened or put on the spot.

Take a moment to brainstorm with him what options are available for behavior in Morning Meeting, then ask him to commit to a new behavior. Tell him to enjoy his lunch and send him off with a smile.

The next day, follow the same routine when you take the children to lunch. You might get to say, "Hey, Connor, I'm so proud of what I saw today." Don't be discouraged if it's necessary to say, "Connor, we made a plan yesterday, but you didn't follow through." Let him know that you feel frustrated or disappointed and you want to know how he thinks you both can solve the problem. Talk it out again and get him to make a new commitment. Take the two minutes to focus on a solution to the problem behavior.

Do this every day for two weeks straight. Identify any positive changes you see and continue to focus on how you and he can work things out. If you invest just a couple of minutes for two weeks, I believe you'll be amazed at the difference. Given the chance, children often learn to revisit solutions that work and to disregard those ideas that don't.

Removal Strategies

Sometimes it's necessary for a child to exit or be removed from a situation or place. I believe that these strategies should be carried out with the benefit of the child, the teacher, and the classroom foremost in your mind.

The Invaluable PKH Note

We all have times when our patience and ability to deal with a child and/or a particular behavior wear thin. Knowing when you're reaching a breaking point is important in avoiding old responses to the child or her behavior. If you're having a tough time mustering the energy to deal with one more episode, you need a backup plan that removes the child from the situation. This gives you a chance to reassess and/or take a break.

I think it's invaluable to have a buddy at school you can depend on. Seek out a teacher you've built a relationship with. Establish an understanding with that person that if you ever send her a child with a Post-it note reading "PKH" (Please keep him), she will keep the student for a while. Each of us—teachers and students alike—must learn to recognize when we need time apart. If we don't, we will end up involved in many, many power struggles.

The amazing thing is that many times the teacher who is on the receiving end of the PKH note may say to you when things calm down, "What was your problem with _____? He was fine in my room." That will remind you that not only do you need breaks from the children, but sometimes the children need a break from their teacher. It seems that often just a change of scenery or a change of the person they interact with can make all the difference.

WHY ANOTHER CLASSROOM IS BETTER THAN THE OFFICE

It's always better to send a child to another classroom than to send her to the principal's office. Many children are a bit like I was as a child: they enjoy the office. No academics take place there. Often the principal is engaged with other duties, and the child is left to sit and eavesdrop. I spent days in the office listening to conversations that were none of my business. I enjoyed sharing these on the playground, as other children were enthralled by information that was supposed to be private.

There were even times when I was in the office and the secretary would give me jobs to keep me out of her hair. I loved making copies on the mimeograph machine; it was noisy and fun to use. Unfortunately, I think that getting to use the mimeograph machine might have been a motivation for me to "earn" my way to the office. (This was probably not what my teacher had in mind when I was sent there!)

If possible, keep a child in an academic environment or with an adult who can help her to find solutions to her problem behavior.

What are a child's choices when a classmate does or says something he doesn't like?

Seclusion, or In-School Suspension

I believe we ought to consider renaming the detention room. We could call it "the room where children go to plot their revenge on the people who sent them there." If a child is sent to a secluded area as a consequence of making certain choices, then I'd suggest that his time in that area should include the following:

- Guidance in understanding and/or identifying why he's been sent there
- Assistance in assessing what occurred and why that behavior isn't appropriate for a classroom
- Communication of the choices that existed and may exist in a similar future situation
- Development of a plan for the future, including a way to build skills that will aid the child in handling a similar situation another time

Finally, if you take a child out of the classroom, you need to have a plan for *returning* him to the classroom.

A Common Cause of Seclusion & a Proactive Solution

In many instances, children are removed and secluded because of inappropriate interactions with classmates. I'm not convinced that these children have learned how to handle situations that involve other people. What are a child's choices when a classmate does or says something he doesn't like? Has the

As teachers our first priority should be to empower children with words and actions.

teacher taken the time to explain to her that this happens in life all the time? Has the teacher helped her to see what her options are when she has issues with other people?

We need to teach children that they have choices and that the choices include the following:

Ignore it. If someone is taunting you or calls you a name, you can choose to ignore it.

Walk away. You may need to remove yourself from the situation.

Wait and cool off. You may need to acknowledge that emotions are high right now and it would be better to wait and address the situation later.

Negotiate or make a deal. Sometimes you may need to negotiate with a classmate—perhaps making a deal for sharing or taking turns. Other times you may need to negotiate space issues.

Talk it out. You may have the option to talk it out. State your case to the other child and explain what you need.

Tell the other person to stop. There may be times when you have to let the other person know that what he's doing is unacceptable and you want him to stop.

Children need to know that they have options for reacting to other children without resorting to retaliation or physical violence. It's not in our power to change someone else. We can't make other people kinder. Instead, we must focus our attention on changing ourselves, and that may mean changing our reactions to the choices others make. As teachers our first priority should be to empower children with words and actions they can use to satisfy their needs.

Physical Intervention

Physical intervention should always be the last resort, something you turn to only when you believe the child is about to hurt himself or another person. I can't think of any other reason to physically restrain a child. Having been trained to physically restrain children, I've seen firsthand the effects of such actions. At some level, any restraint teaches a child that the teacher can control him. We want children to learn to control themselves.

If a child chooses to throw a tantrum on the floor and she's not physically hurting herself or anyone else, let her act out her choice. It may be necessary to ignore the behavior, offer a space for the behavior, or redirect the behavior. Ultimately, the child must decide when the behavior will end. I do not believe that this type of situation calls for physical restraint.

Tough Topics

As we turn to the "tough topics"—lying, stealing, and bullying—it's important to take a closer look at how we sometimes guide our young people. Often adult role models set poor examples. Think about the young child who receives a present she doesn't like. All too often we say, "Just tell _____ you like it. You don't have to wear it. If you say anything, it will hurt _____'s feelings, and you'll seem ungrateful." When we say things like this, we're asking the child to lie.

I admit that I've told my own children not to bring up a present or a topic if they don't have something positive to say. But what if the topic comes up? Do we expect them to lie? Do we even encourage it? I think that we should build communication skills that allow children to get out of such a situation without lying. In response to a question about a present I didn't like, I often say, "I appreciate the time and effort you spent on me. You're very thoughtful." Take the focus off the item and place it on the person who gave it. The way children see adults handle these issues can have a profound effect on how they respond.

Remember what we said earlier about empathy? As we look at ways to deal with the toughest behavioral issues, let's address why a child might behave in a particular way and then decide how we might address the situation. Often we label these behaviors as bad and leave it at that. Frequently, however, the motivation behind the behaviors is much more complicated than that. Each child is unique; each situation is different. As the teacher, you're the one best qualified to determine why a child is exhibiting a particular behavior.

Dealing with Lying

A child's decision to lie can be based on a number of factors. Sometimes a child's lie is truly a form of wishful thinking. If a student tells you that his mom is pregnant and you later find out that isn't true, it may be that the child wants a brother or sister so badly that he's decided to make it happen in a pretend way.

Some children lie in an effort to please others. I know this sounds strange, but some children believe that they should lie so that they can make someone else feel better. Have you ever

It's almost as if they fear that if they aren't perfect, you won't like, love, or care about them.

told a friend that she looks good when in fact you're wondering whether she lost her shampoo and soap? Believe it or not, there are times when we actually condone lying by labeling it as "altruistic."

Other children lie because they feel guilty about something they said or did. They don't want to acknowledge that their choice was inappropriate. This can also happen when a child fears that you'll be disappointed by her actions. She can't stand to have you disappointed in her, so she covers up the behavior with a lie.

Avoiding punishment is a strong motivation for not telling the truth. Children who believe that there will be repercussions for their actions will lie to avoid "facing the music."

I feel that one of the saddest motivations for children not telling the truth is the search for unconditional approval. It's almost as if they fear that if they aren't perfect, you won't like, love, or care about them—that they could lose you because of their behavior. They lie in an effort to ensure that you will continue to value them. These children often fear being isolated and alone.

Each of these motivations is different, and you need to respond to each one differently. Different circumstances call for different solutions.

If wishful thinking is the issue, allow children to express their wishes in positive ways through writing and pretending. For children who lie to avoid hurting others' feelings, model

Experience has taught me that there are even parents who refer to stealing as "permanent borrowing."

making a choice to say nothing rather than to tell a lie. Teach tactful ways to communicate when it's not easy to be truthful.

Teach children to accept the consequences or punishments that result from their choices. Role-play situations that require them to own up to their choices and to deal with the results of those choices. It isn't always easy to face people or situations that make us uncomfortable, but it's part of life, and we can learn to handle the challenge.

One of the most important concepts to convey to children who lie is that it's wrong to lie for any reason, but that lying doesn't mean that someone is a horrible person no one cares about. In many cases, if the perpetrator acknowledges her inappropriate behavior and expresses regret rather than telling a lie, she's much more likely to be forgiven. Lying tends to perpetuate problems, not solve them.

Dealing with Stealing

Young children can often show a great lack of self-control. They take what they see because they want it. For a small child, it's "all about me," and that egocentric state can lead to behaviors that the child hasn't thought through.

There are times when children believe it's okay to steal. They've seen this behavior modeled by adults in their lives. When a parent helps himself to drinks left unattended on a hotel buffet table, he's "telling" a child that it's okay to take things that you haven't paid for or that aren't yours. Children who steal often say that they deserve to have the things they steal. Experience has taught me that there are even parents who refer to stealing as "permanent borrowing." If a child can tell you about the times she has witnessed an adult in her life stealing, it's hard to explain to her why stealing is unacceptable.

Some children who steal do so because they like to push the limits. In this case, the behavior is used as a tool for gaining attention or control. Anger, sadness, jealousy, and a range of other emotions can drive a child to take things that don't belong to him. One of the most common motivations for stealing is an attempt to fill a void. It may be that something is missing in the child's life or that he has a need to be heard.

One of our cornerstones is helping children to learn and display self-control. It's necessary to relate self-control to taking things that don't belong to you just because you want to have them. You can teach self-control by pointing to times when you must use self-control yourself. Tell the children when you see something you'd like to have, then ask them what your options are regarding that object.

Dealing with Bullying

Many people believe that bullying behavior hides a bully's secret insecurities. In fact, research has shown that bullies are often confident individuals. They're also impulsive and domineering, and they can't tolerate frustration. These individuals usually lack a sense of empathy for others.

You can't be a bully unless you have a target. Children who are the targets of bullies often appear insecure, weak, and socially isolated. I would venture to guess that many targets started out as quiet and submissive and that their insecurities and isolation have been compounded by the bullying behavior.

If they take something from someone who has more than she needs, it's still stealing.

With these thoughts in mind, you may be able to reduce bullying behavior if you raise awareness of how bullying affects communities. Discuss with students what bullying behavior is. Brainstorm acceptable actions to take when you are bullied. Create a classroom in which understanding and empathy are valued.

Once you've done all that, the most effective ways to deal with bullying behavior are to ensure that there is adult supervision as often as possible and to show zero tolerance for bullying. The traditional approach of punishing bullying doesn't solve the problem. The situation requires addressing the behavior as being inappropriate, discussing *why* it's inappropriate, and supporting the child or community affected by the behavior.

Reducing bullying in our schools also requires the full support of school staff. That means empathy training, teaching peer support skills, and creating an environment that focuses on positive learning and behavior.

The Bigger Picture: Another Look at Lying, Stealing & Bullying

Make sure children recognize that even little lies are lies and that if they take something from someone who has more than she needs, it's still stealing. Bullying others is unkind and unnecessary.

Role-play and share stories and books about the issues. Be prepared to talk about how stealing affects both the person who takes something and the person he takes it from; both have a stake in the behavior. A similar principle applies to lying. Create opportunities for former bullies and grown-ups who were bullied as children to share their stories with the class. I once knew a principal who had been bullied. By contrast, I had bullied others when I was a child. So we decided to team up to role-play for children both sides of the issue. Children need to hear and see the end results of the behaviors they choose.

Finally, to help children understand these issues at a deeper level, discuss with them the meaning of words such as *values, ownership,* and *compassion.* As with so many of the issues we've discussed in this book, better understanding can be a key to better behavior.

AFTERWORD

Children are our future. As teachers we have the ability to touch the future in ways foreign to most professions. In a single career, each of us has the opportunity to touch hundreds of children's lives. Each word we say and each action we choose may be internalized by a child for years to come. We may never truly know what we've meant to a child. It may take years for the child to understand and recognize it himself.

I've often thought about the teacher I believe changed my life: Joseph Tourville. He was a man who valued education and children. Looking back, I remember that he was hard on me—but in a good way! I remember him as an adult who liked to say, "Donna, you make choices—some good, some bad. You'll have to learn to be responsible for those choices." He always finished with, "Please try to make the best choices you can."

Mr. Tourville helped me to believe that the power lay within me to change the choices I made and that I could, at any time, choose to be a better person and part of a community. Sure, not all of his life lessons were clear to me as a child, but as an adult I truly understand the message he tried so desperately to share. I'm a better person for having had Mr. Tourville in my life. One teacher can change a child's life forever. I know this to be true because one teacher changed mine.

RESOURCES

Charney, R. S. 2002. *Teaching children to care*. Rev. ed. Greenfield, MA: Northeast Foundation for Children.

Coloroso, B. 2002. *Kids are worth it! Giving your child the gift of inner discipline*. Rev. ed. New York: HarperCollins.

Coloroso, B. 2003. *The bully, the bullied, and the bystander: From preschool to high school—how parents and teachers can help break the cycle of violence*. New York: HarperCollins.

Deci, E. L., R. Koestner, and R. M. Ryan. 1999. A meta-analytic review examining the effects of extrinsic rewards on intrinsic motivation. *Psychological Bulletin* 125, no. 6 (November): 627–68.

Deci, E. L., R. Koestner, and R. M. Ryan. 1999. The undermining effect is reality after all: Extrinsic rewards, task interest, and self-determination. *Psychological Bulletin* 125, no. 6 (November): 692–700.

Kohn, A. 1993. *Punished by rewards.* New York: Houghton Mifflin.

Mendler, A. N. 2005. *Just in time: Powerful strategies to promote positive behavior.* Bloomington, IN: National Educational Service.

Nansel, T. R., M. Overpeck, R. S. Pilla, W. J. Ruan, B. Simons-Morton, and P. Scheidt. 2001. Bullying behaviors among US youth: Prevalence and association with psychosocial adjustment. *Journal of the American Medical Association* 285, no. 16: 2094–2100.

Olweus, D. 1993. *Bullying at school: What we know and what we can do.* Cambridge, MA: Blackwell Publishing.

Wood, C. 1997. *Yardsticks.* Greenfield, MA: Northeast Foundation for Children.

INDEX

Also by Donna Whyte

Dinosaurs, Popcorn, Penguins & More

Dinosaurs, Popcorn, Penguins & More CD

The More Ways You Teach, the More Students You Reach
(with Char Forsten, Gretchen Goodman, Jim Grant & Betty Hollas)

Morning Meeting, Afternoon Wrap-Up

My Seasonal Writing Words

My Writing Folder

My Writing Words

Number Match Games *(cards & game suggestions)*

Pig Pals *(manipulatives & activity booklet)*

Read with Your Smartie

Sing Yourself Smart

Sing Yourself Smart CD

The Top 13 Warning Signs That It's Time to Retire
(with Char Forsten, Jim Grant & Betty Hollas)

Volunteers Are Vital
(with Char Forsten, Jim Grant & Betty Hollas)

What Makes a Good Teacher?

The Writing Coaching Tool

Bring Donna Whyte right to your school for on-site training! *To learn how, call (877) 388-2054.*

You Can't TEACH a Class You Can't MANAGE

You can have the best lesson plans in the world, but when your students are playing desk-to-desk leapfrog in the middle of the classroom, lesson plans aren't much help. You need solutions. Solutions that work. Solutions you can use *now*.

That's exactly what you'll find in *You Can't Teach a Class You Can't Manage*. In this tell-it-like-it-is book, Donna Whyte offers specific strategies for addressing specific management problems, and she doesn't shy away from tough issues such as bullying, lying, and stealing. Her focus, though, is on an even greater challenge: teaching children the skills they need to control their own behavior. Donna knows what works in today's classrooms because she's been there. As she shares her own teaching mistakes and successes with humor and insight, she offers down-to-earth, practical, effective strategies for teaching self-control and appropriate choices.

In these pages, you'll find scores of simple but effective ways to teach children how to

- Take responsibility
- Solve their own problems
- Identify and express feelings
- Distinguish between want and need
- Follow directions
- Make decisions
- Negotiate for what they want
- Get back on track after a bad choice

This book will change the way you look at the "troublemaker" in your class. It will help you stop tearing your hair out! And it will free you up to become the teacher you always wanted to be.

ABOUT THE AUTHOR

As a frequent presenter at conferences and seminars across the country, Donna Whyte is known for her positive attitude, her high energy, and her many practical ideas for educators. She also describes herself as a "childhood troublemaker"! So she speaks from experience as she tells what works both for teachers and for "problem students."

US $18.50
ISBN: 978-1-9...

Crystal Springs
BOOKS
www.crystalsprings.com

A division of SDE
Staff Development for Educators
10 Sharon Road, PO Box 500
Peterborough, NH 03458
1-800-321-0401